MONTANA
Images of the Past

MONTANA
Images of the Past

By
William E. Farr
and
K. Ross Toole

PRUETT PUBLISHING COMPANY
Boulder, Colorado 80301

©1978 by William E. Farr and K. Ross Toole
All rights reserved, including those to reproduce this book, or parts thereof, in any form without permission in writing from the Publisher.

Library of Congress Cataloging in Publication Data

Farr, William E., 1938-
   Montana.

   Bibliography: p.
   Includes index.
   1. Montana—History.   I. Toole, Kenneth Ross,
1920-   joint author.   II. Title.
F731.F37   978.6   78-7408
ISBN 0-87108-514-3

First Edition

1 2 3 4 5 6 7 8 9

Printed in the United States of America

Acknowledgments

On a book such as ours, many, many people have contributed valuable assistance, supporting this lengthy project with their time, information, photographs, and hospitality. We would like to acknowledge their help — to all we owe a great deal.

We are particularly grateful — to Margaret Kingsland of the Montana Committee for the Humanities for her initial and continued support of a photographic venture — to Dale Johnson, University of Montana; Lory Morrow, Montana Historical Society; and Minnie Paugh, Montana State University Library, all of whom as archivists provided timely interest, hours of searching and finally photographs to match a whim — to our collector friends: Al Hooper of Butte, Henry Grant of Hamilton, Al Lucke of Havre, Verna Carlson of Circle, Marvin Presser of Wolf Point, George Sollid of Dutton, and Fred Sherburne of East Glacier, Montana.

A special word is needed for Mrs. Richard Smith of Portland, Oregon who generously loaned her grandfather's photographs and to Mrs. Jean Freese who located, borrowed and sent photographs that otherwise would have been lost to us.

We are also indebted to Constance Bourassa, Editor of the *Montana Historian,* for so much help, including an index — to Sue Rabold, our departmental secretary who presides so incomparably — and to Gerald L. Kling and Karen Hodgson, photographers of the Instructional Materials Service of the University of Montana. They were concerned with photographic excellence as they reproduced images which we presented to them that were almost always less than perfect.

Nor could we forget Dianne Kedro of Pruett Publishing Company. We count ourselves fortunate in having had such interested, careful and professional care in the preparation of this volume. This counsel, moreover, was always positive and cheerful.

To these and many more we offer our warmest thanks.

Contents

Preface — 1

Introduction — 5

Gold To Copper: The Influx — 9

The Richest Hill on Earth — 33

Lumbering and the Lumberjack — 59

Cowboys and Sheepmen — 93

Reservation Indians in Montana — 129

Above All, They Made Homes — 165

The Homesteaders — 195

People Having Fun — 219

How's the Road? — 251

Index — 276

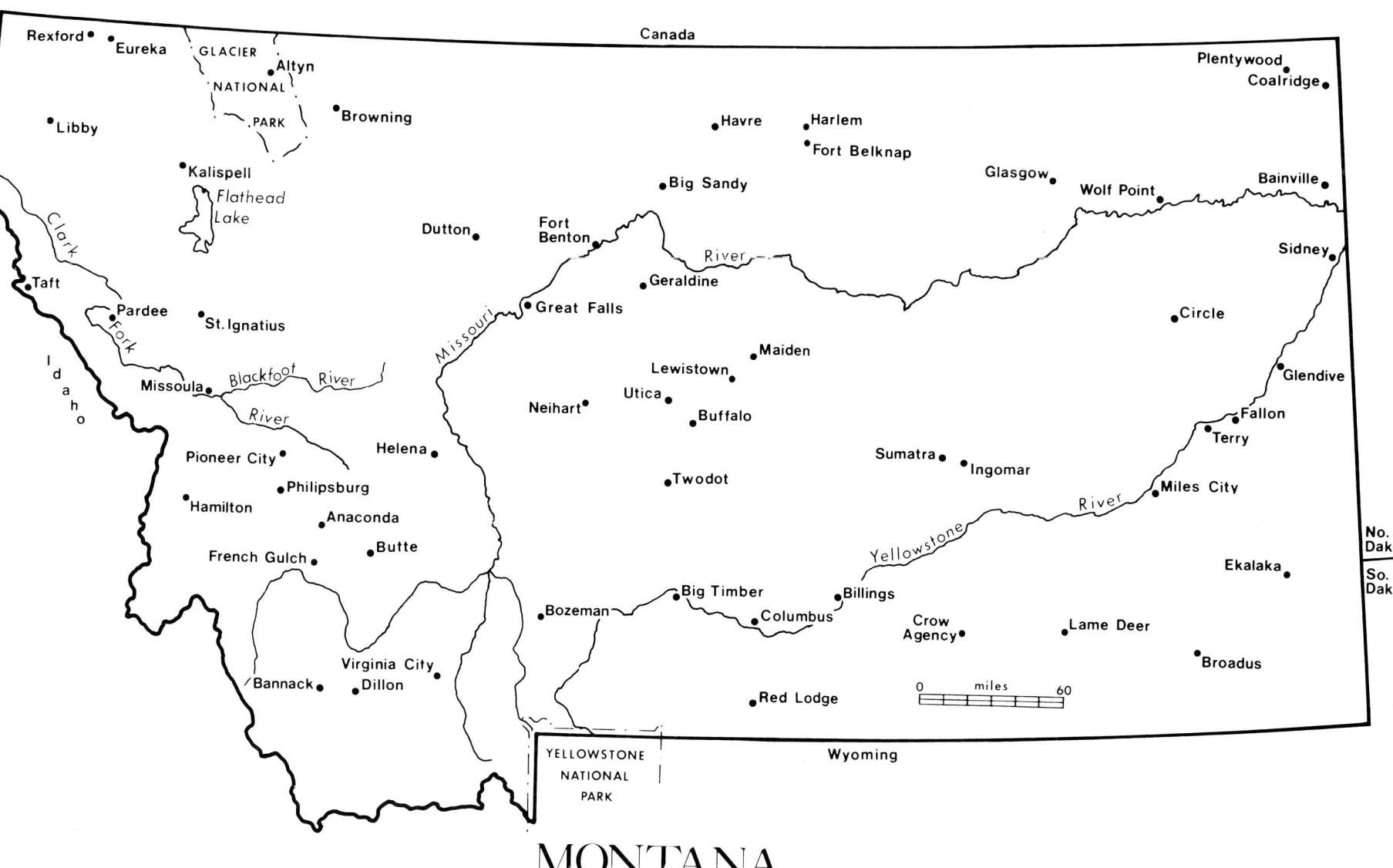

MONTANA

For our Montana kids —

Stefan and Jerusha Farr

*Jon, Jael, Charis, Peter,
Sam, Dana, David Toole*

Preface

This is a pictorial history of Montana. Its purpose, however, is to inform—not to entertain, not to illustrate, not to decorate the polished surface of the living room coffee table, although it may do all of that. It is not, then, simply a picture book. Its goal is to impart information, to render that thin, rich stratum of the historical past in Montana more textured, more meaningful, and more real. We are historians, not photographers, and this volume, because of our backgrounds, has received a different treatment than that of a more usual photographic essay.

Given our historical interest in communicating the presence of the past, we decided very early that contrary to other photographic works, the image and all that it contained had to prevail over the quality of the photograph. The basis for selection, then, was not print quality, not artistic merit, but the historical information the photograph conveyed. Bluntly, the photograph as a historical document was the measure for inclusion. That meant that print quality was sacrificed at times for veracity. Photographs are sometimes rough, imperfect, grainy, and lacking in contrast—but they are always genuine, and they depict the past honestly with revealing, if not beautiful, pictures.

The historical necessity of concentrating on image squared nicely with our determination to present as broad a spectrum of historical photographs as possible—whether taken by professional, talented amateur, or occasional "snap-shooter." Other photographic treatments have often centered on individual photographers, presenting a small, but highly perfected, set of visual gems. Yet their perfection alone renders them unduly selective, artificial, and much too narrow to lay bare the detailed tapestry of historical life in Montana.

Our interest, on the other hand, was to survey, if only briefly, the whole of Montana's unique photographic heritage. That heritage we soon discovered was not contained in a few major depositories such as the archives of the University of Montana, Montana State University, or the Montana Historical Society. Instead it was scattered throughout the state in small museums, smaller private collections, and in a thousand individual hands. Surfacing in a superabundance of shapes, sizes, and conditions, these photographs needed to be preserved; and, because trunks and filing cabinets filled with "old photos" went to city and county dumps, because glass plate negative collections were even transformed into greenhouse panes, there was a sense of urgency.

The Montana Committee for the Humanities and the Hammond Fund of the University of Montana generously supported a large share of the cost, enabling hundreds of photographs, previously lost or unavailable for historical use, to be copied and filed for future use. People from across the state who were interested in history and who had collected local photographs for years, often without recognition and without support, now supported our effort without reserve. Their generosity and willingness to help made this a different and better book.

This campaign to salvage historical, visual documentation opened up a photographic storehouse of novel, unfamiliar images which had seldom, if ever, been seen by the public. They were, in a real sense, rare. And they were culled from thousands of glass plate negatives, old negatives, prints, copies, albums, scrapbooks, and lantern slides. Some came in groups, others singly; they came easily and they came hard. From these we have selected a *very* few which tell *our* story best.

Again, these are not pretty pictures; they are not meant to be. They were not always taken from original negatives or prints; they were copies, or copies of copies, often made years ago and then carelessly. Even when we did come across originals, which in their pristine state had been superb, now those originals were faded or scratched or bent or in some way disfigured.

The caprice of survival and the battering that prints and negatives took were by no means the only limitation to print quality. Early Montana photographers were restricted by their cumbersome equipment and existing technology. Both determined the type of photographs taken as well as the quality of the print image. Only the more adventuresome dared to push their equipment and their ability beyond the primitive mechanical means of the day. R. C. Morrison of Miles City, Montana, was a good example; so was Fred Miller of Hardin. Working on the range at about the same time as the more celebrated L. A. Huffman, Morrison and, later, Miller set about recording flowing, mobile Indians, horses, cowboys, and game, under conditions extreme by any measurement.

Cameras were large, heavy, box-like contraptions which had to be packed, lugged, and somehow set up on ungainly tripods in uncompromising positions. And that was only the beginning, for once set up, these cameras needed a suitable negative. Glass plate negatives were used in a variety of formats to match cameras—4x7, 8x10, 11x14. The really early Montana photographers had only one emulsion at their disposal. It was a "wet" one, an emulsion they poured over the glass plates in a portable darkroom, a tent or wagon, just prior to taking the photograph. Not everyone had the knack or the patience. It required determination and dexterity to carefully tip the plate back and forth, from side to side, to achieve a uniform wash necessary for a clean, evenly exposed negative. The process was troublesome and time consuming, but it was worth it because the resulting negative was more sensitive to light, which shortened the exposure time and made action shots possible.

The wonder is that this special treatment worked at all in the extremes of Montana where Huffman recorded winter buffalo hunters at work in 40 below zero temperatures, and Morrison captured cowboys driving cattle in searing heat and dust. Neither left an account of their experiences with "wet" plates. Their successes add another mysterious dimension to early photographic work.

The actual limitation, then, was not the camera but the negative and its emulsion. It was the emulsion that required the long exposure times to light and thereby prevented the photographer from "stopping" or "freezing" action. Large cameras and "wet" negatives were certainly not convenient, but no one expected convenience. They wanted to photograph a broader range of light, and they wanted to register greater movement.

Only then could they record lives accurately and completely, out of the studio, at work and at play.

Greater emulsion speed and more convenience did come with improvements made in the 1880s. First came an emulsion based on gelatin, which could be used "dry" without any loss of speed. Then ready-made, store-bought, dry glass plate negatives came to Montana, ordered from mail-order supply houses in the East. The new emulsion inaugurated a revolution, for by 1888 George Eastman extended the use of the gelatin base to include a new roll film. With the new film came the "Kodak" camera—light in weight, inexpensive and simple to operate. It became exceptionally popular, and by the turn of the century, everyone was a potential photographer.

In the hands of a professional, the older processes were capable of producing prints of startling clarity, artistry, and depth. Still, although the range of photographic success expanded rapidly, emulsion speed remained a debilitating, limiting factor for most photographers. This in part accounts for the standardized, outdoor, frontal, static, posed, studio pictures we so associate with "old photos." They were not necessary, but they were common. Glass plates cost money; occasions and celebrations were *now* and could not be lost by taking a chance with movement. "Don't move, and say 'cheese'" were the usual admonitions then, and to many, they still are.

There were exceptions, however, and we have tried to find them—adventuresome, experimenting, imaginative photographers who were not satisfied with the conventional, who would not remain within the limitations assigned for safe success. Yet just as they often sacrificed perfection for image, clarity for verisimilitude, so must we.

There is a final consideration for the case of image over quality in a photographic history of Montana. With roll film, the "Kodak" camera, and factory processing, a revolution had transpired, and it did so coincidently with the populating of Montana. Many, many people from every segment of society clicked pictures with "box" and "brownie." These "snap-shot" artists were anything but professional, and their photographs too often reflected the limitations of everyone being a photographer. Print quality fell off astonishingly as photography became more occasional, more popular, and less demanding. But if the quality lessened, there was more of it. And it had a different motive—to record personal, active lives; moreover, it brought with it a different perspective from people whose story only they could tell.

These "snap-shots" were done quickly, easily, often without thought for surroundings, for light or movement or framing. They were not quality images, they were not professional prints, but that did not make them any less historical. For our purposes, they are superb—for they registered a range of activity never before recorded. Whereas professionals and serious amateurs had *created* their image, structuring it, composing it, "snap-shooters" *took* their image as they found it—however bleak, however marred. And as historians confronting that same reality, so too must we comprehend that reality, now historical, in images that are less than perfect.

— William E. Farr

J. C. Morrison drying prints on the sagebrush near Miles City. *Courtesy Mrs. Richard Smith.*

Introduction

Professional photographers, by the last quarter of the nineteenth century, had already made the experiences of the West familiar to Easterners by recording in visual detail the natural, stupifying wonders of both man (the American Indian) and nature (whether the fantastic in Yellowstone or the magnificent in Yosemite). With the technological breakthrough of George Eastman in 1888, great numbers of occasional photographers armed with handy, simple cameras labored to capture the fleeting images of Montana's late, but rapidly passing frontiers. No longer was it necessary for a few to document discovery in the West. Now the task was for many to verify opportunity, progress, and achievement; and to do so, "beginnings" were recorded—of towns, of homesteads, of community halls, of businesses, and of families.

The emergence of the Montana frontier and the continued development of photography in the West coincided fortuitously. Set against the backdrop of a huge, almost empty, always challenging land, Montana photographers, often infrequent and often nameless, attempted to assign to prints images they believed to be transitory. L. A. Huffman of Miles City expressed the feelings of a good many when he remarked that he had made photographs and thereby saved something of the West. And once it was gone, "it was a dream and a forgetting, a chapter forever closed." These photographic prints would be, however, a legacy—permanent, exact likenesses, portable and, most importantly, repeatable, to be retrieved not once but again and again to remind memory of a reality past. The events and experiences of the West had *not* been a dream. They need not be forgotten. It was remarkable insight. Photographers succeeded in registering the nuance of a vanished society.

As often as not, the most imaginative, daring, creative photographers were the amateurs, the "snap-shot" artists whose purpose was not a focused, pretty, perfected saloon print or a starchy, upright portrait. They wanted active, alive pictures of people, their people, doing something. In any case, whether amateur, semiprofessional or professional, Montana experiences were documented on negative after negative—cowboy stag dances, Black minstrel shows, playing catch, busting sod, killing gophers, digging coal, or dragging bottoms. If it was done, it was photographed.

This capacity to freeze, to preserve, and to recover countless moments, motions, and mental states pushed many people into a frame of reference that can only be described as historical. There was a story to tell. They wanted to record and recapture at will their "beginnings," their lives and their efforts, and, once they did, they came to see themselves and their experiences in

Montana in an entirely different light, with a heightened awareness of their uniqueness which in turn rendered them historically significant.

Once these immigrants, foreign and domestic, had presence, were significant and of moment, so too was their history. But they needed a *new* document—a *new* method to record that history. Often these Montanans had had little experience with the written word. Often they felt inhibited by their speech, whether because of foreign birth, accent, or education. These people *saw* in the novel invention of George Eastman—roll film for cameras—a means of establishing their own histories, of writing their own histories in a visual medium. Every family, however limited its resources, could now possess a history. History would not be limited to the literary and the literate. And countless family albums were constructed, portraits taken, and times and places noted and memorized. In doing so, the circle of Americans for whom history was important grew—expanded significantly, meaningfully, by an invention not unlike the family "Ford." Both were readily accessible, cheap, not too demanding to operate successfully and, above all, enlarging in experience and horizon.

Yet in Montana and elsewhere, this cornucopia of visual information too often has languished dormant and unused by historians. This mysterious lack of use is puzzling. Certainly professional historians involved in teaching and research have been worshippers of the written, contemporary document. We are trained to deal with written documentation—letters, ledgers, diaries, newspaper accounts, and legal agreements. These are considered "primary material," closer to the events we are trying to comprehend than anything else and therefore more trustworthy, better evidence in the detective enterprise the historian embarks upon when trying to understand the past. The use of written documentation as evidence has severely limited the historian, blinded him, to other sources of information every bit as reliable. Nowhere is this more demonstrable than with the visual statements contained in historical photographs.

Photographs are indeed documents. To be sure they have to be "read," to be interpreted, just as do written documents. But just as surely, they evidence or verify in ways that are significantly the same. This is by no means self-evident. Historians have made little use of "old pictures." If they used them at all, it was in a decorative sense, to add a "feeling" to the written word. Or they used them as afterthoughts, throwing a few images in here or there, with the location sometimes bearing upon the text, sometimes not. What is needed for historians to continue their creative task of historical reconstruction—and it is coming—is an expanded definition of verifiable evidence, one that will include the visual record.

Other considerations, too, help account for the historians' reluctance to use photographs. The historian, while researching specifically, writes generally. He is forced to generalize—the local historian more than anyone else has been taught to relate the specific to the general in an effort to escape the dreaded, mortal sin of being insignificant, of being an antiquarian. The result has been an important loss of historical reality; for the detail that distinguishes, that identifies, that marks out time and place, is filtered out only to be replaced by a stereotype or outline figure without bone or gristle. Photographs have such detail—in superfluity—a wealth of focused, legible, enumerating particulars that make past experience pungent with life and stinging in its reality. In fact, historical photographs have too much detail, too many sharply defined packets of information to be easily controlled through the process of abstracting a general statement or rule. It is this very surfeit of detail which integrates the photograph, locking it together into an intransigent, stubborn whole, making it difficult indeed to surgically segment the photograph—

then reassemble into a generalization. Yet it is just through such interpretive fiction that historians comprehend the past. Consequently all too often historians have ignored or rejected the visual artifact as too narrow and particular in its description to be of general significance.

"To see is to believe"—medieval scholastics and mystics knew that, and so did early-day Montanans. They wanted to see, to be convinced that progress was possible, that steam could alter the face of eastern Montana, that Cheyenne Indians were both human and personal, that rail transportation could excuse distance. To prove it was to see it, and photographers proved it, telling their stories on film with good pictures, poor pictures, mediocre pictures, but above all, *in* pictures. Like all storytellers, including historians, these picture-takers had biases, a point of view and a point to tell. When photographing the young man east of Havre in 1915 with his new wife, his new homestead, and his new car, the photographer hoped to record the beginnings of a personal odyssey, a sense of optimism that "we can make it;" he also recorded much more. Inadvertently, as the shutter clicked, the neutral lens registered objectively a world of subtle detail—how the homestead shack was built, how it differed from others, how sod had been piled up on the windy side to insulate, how the couple dressed for their wedding, as well as the fact that with the car, a Model T Ford, this homesteader was already a commuter. Working in town and "on the place," he drove back and forth, in "gumbo" with chains, in dust without. All that and more can be "seen" if we "read" photographs patiently and critically, aware of both the intentional and the unintentional in the exchange of information provided by the photographer and his work.

But we knew little of this when we undertook the task of providing a photographic history of Montana. Certainly we recognized the need, and we perhaps divined something of the historical value of photographs, but we also thought it would be simple. First of all would come the text. After all, K. Ross Toole writes about Montana history extensively; and neither of us were strangers to working with documents—varied, voluminous, intensive. It should be simple. Little research should be required; it had been done. The narrative section preceding the photographs could be short. The difficulty would be in finding photographs to illustrate in fitting fashion the narrative. It did not work.

The photographs I had gathered so diligently with the help of so many people did not fit the narrative. Generalizations began to burst with increasing frequency. For instance, Professor Toole had written of the homesteaders' frontier from literary accounts. Since there were hundreds of references to bitter cold, to a ubiquitous scissoring wind, and a few references to burning buffalo chips or fence posts in the cast-iron stove, the conclusion seemed clear. One of the fiercest hardships of the homesteader was the lack of fuel, and that view has been chronicled at length. But as we sifted through hundreds of homestead photographs, we discovered that piles of coal beside the shack were common; so too were pictures of men, women, and their families digging their winter supply of coal in dark seams close to the surface. In fact, the eastern Montana homesteader, more often than not, had little to worry about with respect to fuel.

In other ways, the method of attaching photos to text failed. The visual statement was greater than the sum of its parts—the picture had an integrity which made it difficult to be selective. Something was wrong. We thought to show, for instance, the reservation Indian in the squalor and degradation in which they long existed. That degradation is abundantly evident when considered statistically (tribal statistics, Bureau of Indian Affairs statistics, HEW statistics, etc.). The statistics are appalling, and they are accurate enough. The narrative was written on that basis, and the process of choosing the photographs began.

The method, however, was wrong. Only by deliberately deleting the most *typical* of the photographs could we make the narrative and the photographs square with one another. Only by seeing parts of pictures and suppressing others could the text be supported, and even then with difficulty. The photographs of reservation Indians told a different story than the statistics, for the photographs reflected the spirit, the tenacity, and the survival of Indian identity in a way that statistics could not. The photographs insisted upon it.

We will not burden you with the problems which ensued except to say that we had to reverse accepted procedure entirely. First we learned to study the visual documentation—intently—and *then,* we wrote the narrative. That was a discovery for us, and it taught us an important lesson; the historian who does not use photographs extensively *in his research* (not necessarily including them in his book at all) is leaving a magnificent research source untapped.

In any event, our simple book proved to be quite otherwise. If it was unsettling for us, it was also exciting and rewarding. We hope that some of that feeling is transmitted to the reader.

We do not propose to substitute this photographic history of Montana for any other history. Pictorial histories are not superior to, nor should they replace, narrative history. This is not revisionism. What we hope for is that this book will enliven the dramatic, often quixotic, and always engaging history of this state. It should provide an extra dimension. Montana's visual heritage is rich, and it is rewarding—rewarding to all interested in understanding a mode of living unique to remote, almost empty land far to the north of the great east-west trails, a land which has always encountered too quickly and too late the successive waves of American expansion.

What follows is a communication with the past, a communication that is not based upon words, but upon pictures. Mrs. Verna Carlson of Circle, Montana, remarked when she lent me a set of hauntingly striking photographs that spanned the life of the frontier:

> I thought they had only sentimental value to me as reminders of a simple way of life that I enjoyed. I am glad if you can put some of it into words.

We have not, but it is our hope that the following photographs—immediate, visceral, evocative—will bestow upon you the same sense of place, belonging, and continuity, of pride, survival, and optimism which they have given to Verna Carlson, a representative of so many Montana pioneers.

William E. Farr

K. Ross Toole

September 1977

Gold To Copper: The Influx

The gold frontier was a frontier that moved largely from west (California) to east. By 1858, there were literally thousands of disappointed California gold seekers. The good claims had been staked out; the boom was about over. Disgruntled men fanned out northward and eastward. They penetrated into Colorado and Nevada, into British Columbia, eastern Oregon, Washington, Idaho—and Montana. There is no way to estimate their numbers or to ascertain how many remote gulches they sampled.

By 1862 the rushes into Nevada, Colorado, and even Idaho had begun to peter out. The prospectors, in any event, were always poised to move restlessly onward—and move they did, into Montana.

Undoubtedly the real credit for the discovery of gold in Montana must go to two brothers, James and Granville Stuart. They were returning, disgusted, from the California gold fields in 1858, sank a shaft just east of Missoula (Gold Creek), and found gold.

Yet, though the Stuarts "worked" this discovery, and though it has often been claimed that this was the magnet that drew thousands of gold seekers into Montana, there is no evidence that such was the case. Little gold was taken from this area in spite of the growth of the small community, American Fork, at Gold Creek (then called Benetsee Creek). There is, then, no causal relationship between the Stuarts' discovery and the three real rushes—Bannack, Alder Gulch, and Last Chance Gulch.

The first great strike was on Grasshopper Creek, a tributary to the Beaverhead River, and the town of Bannack was born. By mid-winter of 1863, there were about 500 people in Bannack, living in wickiups, tents, and the crudest of board and log structures. By spring, Bannack had a roistering population of about one thousand.

Then, as these restless men moved onward, came the other great strikes. Alder Gulch, or Virginia City, was next. This discovery in the Ruby Valley temporarily depopulated Bannack. It was incredibly rich, and by the fall of 1863, the long gulch had spawned not only Virginia City but also Nevada City, Circle City, and Central City.

If you had climbed the hill behind Virginia City in 1864 and looked down the gulch you would have seen a chaotic sight. Six thousand people, almost all young men, were digging, pushing, sluicing, cursing, and fighting. Teams and heavy wagons jammed the gulch bottom, and the road, if such it could be called, was hub deep in mud from rain and obscured by dust when the road dried. Its ruts and furrows were knee deep.

Up to your right you could see the plumes of steam and smoke from a sawmill, turning out green boards as fast as the crew could feed logs into the whirling, belt-driven saws.

Teams hauling logs, buildings going up, tents everywhere. And noise, the noise of 6,000 men all in a hurry; a hurry to dig, to build, to haul, to fight, to drink—and all in a hurry to get rich—and fast. Not the stereotyped, old bearded prospector with his laden burro, not that at all. Young men, many in their teens, tough men. Men from California, the experienced hands, but also men from the South, ex-Confederates. Men from farms, the cities—and men from China. The gulch was deep, and so the noise echoed and re-echoed, a kind of sustained cacophony. That was Alder Gulch in 1864.

The rumors boiled in bars and hostels. New strikes—a great one up on the Kootenai River. And the restless men spun off again. Four of them, later to be called "the Four Georgians," headed for the Kootenai strike. They met discouraged miners returning from there, remembered a promising looking gulch they had left behind—and turned back. Prickly Pear Creek was their last chance. On July 4, 1864, they hit it. Last Chance Gulch—and Helena was born, repeating the scene in Alder Gulch.

There would be little merit in chronicling each new strike and rush. Suffice it to remark that by the early 1870s, there were some 500 gold-bearing gulches—and in each, its town or towns were almost invariably called "City"—Butte City, Diamond City. No villages here, no towns. Cities they were—or if they were not, they would be. Pretention? No. An ebullient, crackling, roaring optimism.

It is important to emphasize the difference between "placer" and "quartz" mining, because the former takes very little capital, but the latter takes a great deal. Placer mining, in effect, involves surface or near-surface gold, and the gold is "pure" in the form of nuggets or "dust." "Pure" is really not a good word to use, because gold, especially "dust," varies widely in purity, and that purity was measured on a scale of "0 to 900 fine."

The point is that placer mining did not involve gold imbedded in rock or "quartz." Though the miner did, indeed, have to dig, in addition to panning, this was pick-and-shovel work. The gold-bearing earth was shoveled into a "rocker," which was a box with a screen on top so that rocks could be scraped off. The rocker was then rocked back and forth as water was poured in. The earth moved from the rocker down into sluice boxes, which were simply long, flume-like structures. At the bottom of the sluices there were riffles, or small boards, tacked or nailed every few inches or so. As the wet earth was first rocked and then sluiced down the flumes, the gold, being much heavier than the other material, dropped to the bottom and was caught on the riffles.

This was a primitive method, indeed. But it worked. All the equipment a man needed was a pan—usually used to find "colors," or a promising site—a pick, a shovel, an axe, a saw, and a great deal of muscle. The early rushes into the Rocky Mountain West were placer rushes—and let it be emphasized again that this endeavor required very little capital.

Placer mining was a very ephemeral business and, rich as the areas were, they were rather quickly played out. Often a town (city) was a ghost town within a year or two. Sometimes sooner. But placer gold is very often found in association with "quartz gold," and the gold period does not end with the end of the placer period. For quartz gold, the miner must tunnel, follow the veins, and shore up his tunnel with strong wooden beams. Moreover, he must blast the quartz loose and then crush it to separate the gold. This involved "stamp mills" or crushing mills—and this meant capital. You had to have large structures, boilers, fuel, employees, and heavy equipment.

Fort Benton on the Missouri River was one of the few fur-trading posts that had survived. In the 1840s and 1850s, it was a sleepy little community. Then it became Montana's most important community. Indeed, it was one of the most important communities for the northern Rocky Mountain West. Why? Because the overland routes to Montana were long, dangerous, and slow. But paddle-wheel steamboats could reach Fort Benton from St. Louis—with luck, in only thirty-five days. The boats could carry heavy material which could be freighted in the giant ox- or horse-hauled freight wagons to Helena, Butte or, for that matter, all the way to Walla Walla, over the military's newly constructed Mullan Road.

Certainly, the steamboat season was short—at best, three months. The freight charges were very high indeed. But it was worth it. In placer gold alone, Montana had produced $90,800,000 from 1862 to 1876. And the "quartz" era was coming into its own. Silver strikes were also occurring, and silver, like quartz gold, required heavy equipment.

In order to get a clear idea of what was happening in Montana, therefore, Fort Benton is the window through which to peer.

From 1866 to 1868, laden to the gunwales, the boats rushed up the river: thirty-one in 1866; thirty-nine in 1867; thirty-five in 1868. In 1867 alone, they carried 8,061 tons of freight to Fort Benton, as well as 10,000 people. A steamboat could net $80,000 in a single season. Fort Benton's levee towered with boiler parts, boxed goods, bales, barrels, weapons, kegs, sacks, and its warehouses bulged with foodstuffs, clothing, furniture, whiskey, and every imaginable kind of equipment. A single steamer in the year 1867 carried $1,250,000 worth of raw gold to St. Louis.

The railroads were probing very, very slowly westward and northward toward Montana. They were not to reach it until 1883. Until they did, Fort Benton was far and away the most important hub of a huge empire. In the late 1860s and early 70s, it was not unusual for thirty-five or forty steamboats, with their boiler safety valves tied down, to be racing up and down the river. From Fort Benton, the great freight trails radiated northward into Canada, northwestward into Washington, and westward to the mining cities.

It will not do to leave the gold rush era without some comments about government, law, and social community. In some respects there is a mystery here. The records we have indicate a history of raw violence, lawlessness, and summary justice. This is the picture we get in Thomas Dimsdale's *Vigilantes of Montana* (who was there); it is the picture we get in Nathaniel P. Langford's *Vigilante Days and Ways* (he was himself a vigilante). Stemming from these few sources, many subsequent writers have elaborated on the theme that mining communities were universally dangerous, anarchic, and without the amenities. Certainly they were no place for a man without a gun, and a man not only skilled in its use but willing to use it on almost any pretext. Is this an accurate picture? No, it is wildly distorted.

It is true that Henry Plummer and his band of about thirty desperadoes (who called themselves the "Innocents") murdered some 102 persons between the winters of 1862 and 1864. It is true that the Vigilantes, a group of very courageous and determined men, formed into a tightly knit organization, and between December 21, 1863, and January 11, 1864 (less than one month), they hanged thirty-four "Innocents," including Henry Plummer. But this was not a random, "Ox-Bow Incident" type of activity. They had a complete list of the outlaws, provided by one of the "Innocents," Red Yeager, who had been captured early in the hunt. They had a list of the specific crimes committed by each and not one of the men charged with these crimes proclaimed his innocence.

But there is more to it than that. Let us view, with

appreciation, the works of Dimsdale and Langford, for these are accurate and splendid accounts. But let us also dig a little deeper, because there *are* other sources. How does it happen that an educated and observant man, J. H. Morley, lived in Virginia City during the entire period and kept a meticulous diary covering innumerable subjects—and never once mentioned a road agent, a murder, or a Vigilante?

The facts would seem to be that the ordinary citizenry of these communities went peacefully about their business, unarmed, and were simply too busy to take note of what we today conceive of as being the principal characteristic of the time and place—violence. There *was* violence; it was *not* predominant.

Government was extraordinarily streamlined, simple, and effective. By that statement, we do not refer to territorial government which was superimposed from Washington and which was often ludicrous and seldom effective. Indeed, we shall not even consider territorial government (1864–1889) in this book, because it is simply too low on the priority list. A single comment will have to suffice. Territorial government worked not at all or, at best, feebly, because—and note—it was devised in the East by men who did not understand the West and its peculiar needs and circumstances.

But what of the government that was devised here? When a gold strike occurred, the populace in common marked off the physical boundaries of the "district." That was the unit of government. The people then elected a president, a recorder, a sheriff, and a court. The usual term was six months. After all, these were practical people, and there might not even *be* a "district" six months hence.

The first task of government was to assign claims within the district. In this process, there were variations from district to district. But when assigned, the claim was recorded. The second task was meticulously to apportion water, per claim. This was vital because one could not mine without water. Water was measured out in miner's inches. Woe now to the claim jumper or the water thief—because there *was* a court.

In some districts, a man might have more than one claim. The officials also determined what length of time a miner could be absent from his claim without losing it, and how much work he had to do to keep it. In other words, there was to be no land speculation. And there was none.

The Miner's Court was a powerful institution. It tried both civil and criminal cases. Attorneys were permitted on both sides. Rules of evidence consisted largely of common sense rather than precedent. Usually there was a jury, and its nature, again, varied from district to district. In some districts, in criminal cases, the accused had the right to choose either a jury impaneled by the court, or he could stand before the populace of the entire district, who would vote on his guilt or innocence.

Criminal law was not very complex. Jails existed but were not often used. Punishments were public flogging (rare), banishment from the district (very common), or death (rare except for the Vigilante period).

That, then, was the structure of government—and it was very effective. It was based on the particular needs of the people of a district and on the philosophy that government should confine itself to those particular needs and involve itself in no others. It worked.

Certainly, as the economy evolved and "cities" took on at least the aura of permanence, other structures had to be devised—and they were. There is a kind of anomaly, however, in the fact that territorial government and "local" government existed side by side—and, by and large, ignored each other. A very common view of the "imported" government, often expressed in the newspapers of the day, was mild contempt. The contempt *was* mild because, after all, it did not matter much. These were a very practical people, and they were very busy. What worked was what mattered to them. What did not work, they strongly tended to ignore.

By the middle seventies, there was something of a depression in Montana. In many areas, such as Butte, the gold had run out—or, its mining was complicated because of the presence of silver. Silver was valuable, all right, but these were gold miners.

There was another problem in Butte which dated back at least to 1865. The gold miners, and then the silver miners, were constantly plagued by the presence of copper. When copper ore encounters water and air, it oxidizes. No matter where a shaft was sunk in Butte and environs, this green stuff had to be dealt with; it had to be hauled away and dumped somewhere. Its presence fouled up the workings of the silver stamp mills. It was always in the way.

And copper? Who wanted copper? These men were miners of precious metals. Copper was certainly not a precious metal. You made pots and pans out of it—and the copper mines of Spain and those in Michigan were already producing enough copper to satisfy the pot and pan makers forever.

Butte already had its silver problem. It was, in fact, very discouraging to have this copper problem added to all of the others.

Virginia City, Montana Territory. Jackson Street looking south, late 1860s. *Courtesy Montana Historical Society.*

Washing to bedrock in Alder Gulch, Montana Territory, ca. 1870. *W. H. Jackson, photographer; Hayden Survey, 1869-71. Courtesy Montana Historical Society.*

Panning for nuggets and dust. Alder Gulch, Montana Territory, 1870. *W. H. Jackson, photographer; Hayden Survey, 1869-71. Courtesy Montana Historical Society.*

The prospector and his tools. Alder Gulch, Montana Territory, 1870. *W. H. Jackson, photographer; Hayden Survey, 1869-71. Courtesy Montana Historical Society.*

Last Chance diggings in the early years. Helena, Montana Territory, ca. 1875. *Courtesy Montana Historical Society.*

Supplying the goldfields. Fort Benton Levee, Fort Benton, Montana Territory, 1879. *Courtesy Montana Historical Society.*

Gold miner with rocker in Grasshopper diggings. Alder Gulch, Montana Territory, ca. 1870. *W. H. Jackson, photographer; Hayden Survey, 1869-71. Courtesy Montana Historical Society.*

A mining metropolis. Highland City butcher shop. Helena, Montana Territory. *Courtesy Montana Historical Society.*

Sluicing for gold, 1870. *W. H. Jackson, photographer; Hayden Survey, 1869-71. Courtesy Montana Historical Society.*

Hydraulic head in Nelson Gulch near Helena, Montana, 1905. *Courtesy Montana Historical Society.*

Pioneer City, 1863. *Courtesy University of Montana Archives.*

Helena, Montana. Urban center of the mining community. *Courtesy University of Washington Archives.*

Sixteen sheriffs of early day Montana. *Courtesy Museum of the Rockies.*

Miners' Union Day Parade in mud. Neihart, Montana, June 13, 1892. *Courtesy William E. Farr.*

The Hanging Tree. Helena, Montana Territory, 1875. *Courtesy Montana Historical Society.*

Freighting to goldfields. Between Fort Benton and Helena, Montana Territory. *Courtesy Montana Historical Society.*

Mining in Glacier National Park prior to its creation. Altyn, Montana, August 25, 1900. *Courtesy Sherburne Collection.*

One-man mining. *Courtesy William E. Farr.*

Main Street from Quartz. Butte, Montana Territory, 1877. *Courtesy Leggat Collection, Montana State University Archives.*

"Finished for the day." Ore cart with tools at No. 9.
Courtesy Al Hooper.

"God never made a better man than Rhenban — when he was sober." Altyn, Montana, ca. 1900.
Courtesy Sherburne Collection.

"Roughing it in a tent-city." Quigley, Montana, 1890-1892. *Courtesy University of Montana Archives.*

Hauling gold ore to the stamp mill in central Montana. *Courtesy Montana Historical Society.*

At the Maginnis Mine and Mill. Maiden, Montana, ca. 1890. *W. H. Culver, photographer. Courtesy Montana Historical Society.*

Hauling wood to the Elkhorn Mine, Boulder, Montana, 1890. *Courtesy Montana State University Archives.*

Hauling boiler from Winifred to Ruby Mine, Zortman, 1915-1916. *Courtesy Museum of the Rockies.*

William Cruse Mill with sixty stamps. Marysville, Montana Territory, July 1884. *Courtesy Montana Historical Society.*

Western Montana mining camp at turn of the century. Pardee, Montana. *Courtesy University of Montana Archives.*

The dream remains — simple tools and hard work can bring a strike, ca. 1910. *Courtesy William E. Farr.*

The Richest Hill on Earth

One hot August day in 1876, a thirty-five-year-old man got off the stagecoach which had arrived in Butte about 4 p.m. from Corrine, Utah. Like the other passengers, he was hot, thirsty, and covered with dust. He beat the dust off his clothing with his hat and, carrying a canvas duffel bag, made his way to the Hotel de Mineral. He was a man of medium height with a rather stocky build, but the most notable thing about him were his eyes, which were intensely blue and steady. The clerk who registered him at the Hotel de Mineral noticed that he had a pronounced Irish brogue. The name on the register was Marcus Daly.

The stagecoach ride from Corrine was a rocking, jarring, swaying, jouncing, and interminable journey. Such rides exhausted "pilgrims." But Marcus Daly was no pilgrim. Long before dark he was prowling around the dump heaps, the hoists, and inspecting the general "mess" that was Butte City—population then about 3,200.

Daly had come from Ireland in 1857 and had spent five years in New York, but what he did there we do not know. In 1861, he arrived in Calaveras County, California—mining country. We do know that he moved on to Nevada and served out an apprenticeship as a "hot water boy" in the steaming sumps of Nevada's great Comstock Mine in the late 1860s. By 1872, he was a roving prospector for Walker Brothers, a mining and banking firm in Salt Lake City. It was in that capacity that he came to Butte in 1876.

From subsequent events, we know a good deal about the nature of this extraordinary man. But it is the events that tell us about him, not Daly himself. There are not more than a dozen letters signed by him in existence. He kept no diary. He had a highly developed sense of privacy—indeed, even of secrecy. But we still know these things about him: he had an uncanny "nose for ore;" he had extraordinary vision; he was generous, witty, and outgoing, but he felt ill at ease in "social circles;" he had a quick temper and a long memory; and he had a consuming curiosity about everything connected with mining. That curiosity was not localized. He read voraciously, and he made it his business to know not merely what was going on in western mining, but what was happening on the metal markets in New York, Boston, and in Europe. It is worth remarking that Marcus Daly had the equivalent of an eighth-grade education.

For Walker Brothers, he bought a silver mine in Butte, the "Alice," taking a one-third interest in it for himself. Between 1876 and 1880, he ran the Alice Mine—and very successfully. So successfully, indeed, that when he sold out his interest in 1880, he received $100,000.

We know from the letters of two bankers and

miners, A. J. Davis in Butte and S. T. Hauser in Helena, that in early 1877 Daly was up to something very peculiar. He was exhibiting a great curiosity about copper. This puzzled Hauser and Davis who, in a fascinating exchange of letters, exhibited their respect for Daly but wondered why any miner would really be interested in copper.

With his money from the Alice Mine, Daly bought a small mine (its shaft was only sixty-five feet deep) on top of the great russet hill beneath which the town crouched in its ugly gulch. He paid $30,000 for the property, which its owners had named "Anaconda." That left him with $70,000 to develop the prospect, and in 1880, that was a great deal of money. But for what Daly had in mind, that was a drop in the bucket. He needed *real* money. The question, of course, is what *did* he have in mind? He himself leaves us no key, but others do.

Back in 1872 in Utah, Daly had met George Hearst (father of William Randolph Hearst), who was working as a roving prospector for a strange and fabulously wealthy San Franciscan named James Ben Ali Haggin. The two men (Daly and Hearst) fell to gossiping, and Hearst asked Daly if he had seen any worthwhile prospects. Daly said that as a matter of fact, he had, and he had recommended one to Walker Brothers, but they had turned it down. Daly told Hearst that he ought to look it over and recommend it to Haggin. Hearst did, and Haggin bought the property. This was to become the great Ontario mine, which by 1881 had netted Haggin $18 million. Hearst, as was customary, was in on the action. Neither Hearst nor Haggin forgot Marcus Daly.

By then, Daly wanted money to develop the Anaconda, and a letter to Hearst brought it. It also created a partnership of Daly, Haggin, Hearst, and one Lloyd Tenis—and the "Anaconda Gold and Silver Mining Company" was born. Note the name. No copper is mentioned, but Daly was by now more than mildly interested in copper.

In 1882, Daly wrote Hearst that he had plans for Anaconda and that he wanted the partners to come to Butte. Hearst and Haggin came. Tenis did not. For what happened then we rely, again, on events—but we also rely on George Hearst's memoirs. This section of the memoirs is striking, because what took place then utterly shocked and confounded George Hearst.

Daly took them down the main shaft, then about 400 or 500 feet deep, then led them off in the drifts running out laterally from the shaft. Hearst asked questions about the diminishing veins of gold and silver. James Ben Ali Haggin was a very taciturn man, and he asked no questions at all.

They ascended the shaft, and the three men then sat down in the cool shadows of the gallow's hoist. Remember, now, what they could see from the hill. Butte was served by no railroad. They were looking off over a vast, spiney-hilled wilderness. Below them, the town was hardly impressive. Though things were, indeed, picking up in silver (the area produced nearly $8 million in silver that year, compared to less than $3 million in gold), Butte was still a dirty, dump-heap of a little town, remote and transient looking, squatting in a huge, empty, and extraordinarily rugged country. The only way in or out was by stagecoach and by the great-wheeled freight wagons—and then only when the weather permitted. It was in this context that Daly laid out his plan.

What they had just seen, he told them, was copper ore running about thirty-five percent pure. They were, in fact, he said, sitting on an enormous mountain of copper. He had studied it; it would not peter out.

To an increasingly incredulous Hearst, he then proposed that they build the world's largest and most advanced copper smelter; it could not be built in Butte because of inadequate water, but hopefully would be built somewhere nearby. That, of course, would require the building of a new city—and that, in turn, would require the building of a railroad to ship the ore from Butte to the smelter. Since the most advanced smelters were in Swansea, Wales, he proposed the immediate importation of several hundred Welshmen to construct and run the new smelter. Butte was neither a gold nor a silver camp. It was a copper camp—and it would become a great copper city.

George Hearst was flabbergasted. The questions poured out. Copper was worth only about twenty-four cents per pound. How did Daly figure to compete with the Michigan copper mines which were smelting pure native copper (huge nugget-like chunks not imbedded in rock)? Michigan had the cheapest transportation in the world—barges on the Great Lakes—while Butte, even when the railroad arrived, would have 1,200 miles of costly overland haulage. And for such a huge smelter, where would the fuel come from? Where was the coal? Where were the huge timber operations which would be required for both the mine and the smelter? All of the sawmills in the territory could not provide the needed timber and fuel. And what of the market? Michigan controlled the copper prices through a syndicate of Boston banks.

Patiently, Daly answered each of the questions in detail. Montana had all of the timber that could ever be needed. Yes, the company would have to go into the lumbering business on a very large scale. Montana also had coal—lots of it. Yes, they would have to bring it in. He proposed to handle the Michigan price situation by pushing such vast amounts of copper onto the market that Michigan and Boston could not set the price.

Then Daly put it all in perspective. He said that though the citizens and miners of Butte probably did not know it, an economic revolution was taking place. It was an electrical revolution—and that meant copper, the best conductor of all. That meant wire. That meant armatures. If you read the technical journals, he said, you could see that the revolution was not merely on the horizon; the year was 1882, and the revolution was *here.* Copper was also coming into its own as a building material. It made the best roofing in the world. You could not make brass without copper. Yes, the whole operation would take huge sums of money. But there would also be huge profits.

Hearst heard Daly out and then said, "I cannot go for this. I am a gold and silver man. I want nothing to do with copper." But the senior partner was James Ben Ali Haggin. Inscrutable, half Turkish, the owner of about half of San Francisco, the arbiter of all social matters on Nobb Hill, the owner not only of the great Ontario mine but also of the much greater Homesteak Mine, one of the wealthiest men in America—James Ben Ali Haggin had said nothing. Now, for a long moment, he stared off over the wild country and then slowly turned to Hearst and said, "George, I think we had better go along with Mr. Daly."

Thus the Anaconda Copper Mining Company was formed. And thus the great smelter was built, twenty-six miles to the west, completed by 1884. And thus the new city was built, Anaconda. And thus the Butte, Anaconda and Pacific Railroad was built. And thus great lumbering enterprises sprouted all over west of the divide. And thus the Welshmen came. And thus Butte spurted in population, and all of the bankers and miners who had for so long hated copper rushed into the copper business. Montana was never to be the same again.

The famed Anaconda Mine located on "the richest hill on earth," the Butte hill. Named for the Anaconda snake, this was the mine that changed the orientation of Butte from gold and silver to copper. Butte, Montana, ca. 1890. *Courtesy Al Hooper.*

The expansion of Butte — smelters in 1878, railroad in 1881, copper discovered in 1882. Urban life emerged in Butte, Montana, ca. 1900. *Courtesy University of Montana Archives.*

Neversweat Mine with its seven stacks and wooden headframe sandwiched between the Anaconda and the St. Lawrence. Butte, ca. 1900. *Courtesy World Museum of Mining.*

Mine workers waiting with candles before the Buffalo Mine, Centerville. Candles indicated the length of the shift: two candles for eight hours, three candles for ten. Butte, ca. 1900. *Courtesy Al Hooper.*

Station tender and shaft cages. West Street Mine, Butte, ca. 1900. *Courtesy Al Hooper.*

Triple compartment shafts and double-decked cages of the Portland Mine. Ground level. Butte, Montana. *Courtesy Al Hooper.*

Steam-driven marine type hoist employed at Mountain Consolidated Mine. Butte, ca. 1890. *Courtesy Al Hooper.*

One of the many copper ore smelters, the Montana Ore Purchasing (M.O.P.) Smelter established by F. Augustus Heinze.
Courtesy Montana Historical Society.

Smelter and reduction plant with world's tallest stack. Anaconda, Montana.
Courtesy University of Montana Archives.

Furnaces of United Copper Company Smelter. *Courtesy Montana Historical Society.*

Miners with round lunch buckets. Butte, ca. 1900. *Courtesy William E. Farr.*

F. Augustus Heinze speaking to Butte citizens from steps of Silver Bow County Courthouse. *Courtesy University of Montana Archives.*

W. A. Clark and his lieutenants; from left, Cornelius Kelley, John Ryan, J. Bruce Kremer, and W. A. Clark in front of old Butte High School. *Courtesy Museum of the Rockies.*

Underground at the Pittsmont Mine. Miners with sou'westers on drilling holes for powder with compressed air drill. Butte, Montana ca. 1905. *Courtesy Al Hooper.*

Miners at level 2426. "A great deal of moisture here." Butte, Montana, December, 1908. *Courtesy Al Hooper.*

Slope over 235' level. Black Rock Mine with "Little Wonder" drill. *Courtesy Al Hooper.*

"Shift bosses at noon hour." Butte, 1908.
Courtesy Montana Historical Society.

"Raise men at 2432 feet." *Courtesy Al Hooper.*

Young miner and horse pulling ore car; both have carbide lamps. Butte, ca. 1910. *Courtesy University of Montana Archives.*

Trussing a mule or horse to be lowered underground in miners narrow cage into mine shaft to pull ore cars. *Courtesy World Museum of Mining.*

Drying room before there were showers for the miners. *Courtesy Museum of the Rockies.*

Backyards on the 1100 block of East Broadway. Butte, 1908. *Courtesy Montana Historical Society.*

Elks Convention. Broadway and Main, Butte, ca. 1920. This conventioning elk was made of chicken wire and plaster. *Courtesy William E. Farr.*

Streetcars, wagons, and pedestrians, all at home on the streets of bustling Butte, 1908. *Courtesy World Museum of Mining.*

Miners Union Hall blown up by dynamite on June 13, 1914. *Courtesy University of Montana Archives.*

Crowds near Speculator Mine awaiting news of their loved ones. Speculator Mine disaster, June 8, 1917. *Courtesy World Museum of Mining.*

Concrete crew to "gunnight" wooden shaft supports with mixture of sand, concrete, and water for fire protection. Speculator Mine, Butte, 1918 — one year after the fire disaster. *Courtesy Al Hooper.*

Shafts, drifts, and timbering in the Speculator Mine. Butte, ca. 1920. *Courtesy Al Hooper.*

Columbia Gardens, established in 1899 by W. A. Clark for the people of the mining city. Butte. *Courtesy World Museum of Mining.*

Balloon ascension at Columbia Gardens, 1910. *Courtesy World Museum of Mining.*

Rowing on the lake at the "Gardens" with dance pavilion in the background. *Courtesy World Museum of Mining.*

Senator W. A. Clark with Butte kids at Columbia Gardens. *Courtesy Al Hooper.*

The "Other Butte." Grainy, grimy, and glum. *Courtesy Montana Historical Society.*

Swampers below ventilation pipe, Butte mines. *Courtesy Allan G. Hooper.*

Lumbering and the Lumberjack

I

Man has been cutting down trees since he first developed tools suitable for the job. Often, even with the most primitive of implements, he completely denuded huge stands of timber. Today we consider reference to "the Cedars of Lebanon" as mythological. The reference is factual. The passage from forest to sand dunes was an actual process, and it did not take a millennium.

In spite of hot arguments about forest practices in Montana today, there is little chance now of that sort of thing happening. Whatever the arguments, we do have a basic sustained yield policy, legal restraints on natural resource managers, and a very alert, environmentally oriented public.

Yet we would guess that few Montanans realize that in the first century of lumbering in Montana, we cut about twenty billion board feet—enough to load 10,000 freight trains. Moreover, though today we realize that what we call "the forest products industry" is vital to Montana's economy, few of us realize that lumbering has been a "root industry" for more than a century. Had Montana not been endowed with some 22,354,000 acres of forested land, there could have been, for instance, very little mining. It is difficult to see how the railroads could have been built through the Rockies; it is equally difficult to envision how farmers and ranchers could have functioned efficiently without poles, posts, and ties.

Because so much of Montana's 94 million acres is plains country, and relatively treeless, it is a commentary on our natural wealth that, even so, about 3.5 percent of the total *commercial* forest in the United States is to be found in the mountain areas of Montana.

Even more difficult for us to comprehend today is the nature of lumbering before its mechanization—before tracked caterpillars, logging railroads, bulldozers, trucks, winches, chain saws and, indeed, even balloons and helicopters. To realize how quickly one generation forgets the hardships of another, it is well to remember that, as late as the 1930s, the essential "power unit" in the logging industry was the horse—or, more properly, the horse and the lumberjack. And the task of both was to get the trees down and the logs out of the mountains into the valleys where Montanans lived.

As with the cowboy, we have made the lumberjack into something larger than life. Paul Bunyan: a man of uncommon size and strength, a bearded giant, a roaringly independent symbol of freedom. In the mythology, we not only ill serve the facts, we ill serve the men.

Most of Montana's lumberjacks were of Finnish, Swedish, or Norwegian extraction. The majority were not large men. On the contrary, they were lean, almost to the point of apparent emaciation. They were not "strong men"; they were skilled men, and they had incredible endurance. Their skills, now largely lost to the industry, bordered on artistry. It is a rare Montanan today who has ever seen a double-bitted axe used with the precision of a surgeon's scalpel. But the tool was thus used. So were the peavey, the cant hook, the pike pole, and the crosscut saw.

The sawyers worked in teams; the gleaming, thin saw cut through the trunks of huge trees with a constant, easy rhythm. Easy? Watch two big, strong novices trying to use a crosscut saw today. They strain. The saw binds and bends. The big men sweat. Strength will not prevail. Yet the lean sawyers of, say 1910 to 1940, could saw steadily for ten hours a day, moving quickly from tree to tree, winter and summer. Rhythm, rhythm and artistry. The great tree fell exactly where it was supposed to—not two feet off, one way or the other. In a matter of minutes, another specialist had limbed it with his double-bitted axe, sharp as a razor, flashing up and down. Again, the easy rhythm, the deceptive skill, the surgeon.

Even after the railroads came (1883), the logs were often driven down to the big mills in "river drives." Branch rail lines for logging purposes were built rather slowly. Where streams were handy, therefore, the river drives brought the logs down from the high country. Where streams were non-existent, flumes were built. These were artificial rivers that transported logs off and out of the hills. In either case, water was necessary.

For a log drive, the loggers needed high water—roaring water. Sometimes in a low-water year, they would create high water by backing it up with a series of log dams. Then they would shoot logs down from the mountains into the backwater in great flumes—or drag them down with horses along hand-hewn "skids" in chutes. Then, successively, the log dams were dynamited.

But the mass of logs was sure to "jam" and pile up while the precious water flowed beneath. Enter other specialists. The lumberjack with spiked boots and a long pike pole now took over. He leapt from one moving log to another, pushing, prying, jumping. His first job was to prevent a jam which meant that, like the "point man" on a cattle drive, he was to keep the logs moving. That meant that behind him there were tons of deadly rushing logs. His life depended on his balance, speed, and his skill with the pike pole.

When a jam occurred, the pike pole men were also blasting specialists. Time was short. Dynamite had to be placed strategically to break the jam. Once broken, with a roar and upheaval of logs and water, it was back to the pike pole, to the awesome ballet on the river.

But the logging branch lines did come, and the river drives passed into history, now all but forgotten. No one has bothered to memorialize the pike pole dancers.

What of the logging branch rail lines that ran to the yards? The terrain was steep and rough. So were the roadbeds. No ordinary locomotive would suffice. Enter the stubby Shay locomotive. It was awesomely tough and powerful, but it was not built for speed. Its pistons ran vertically to each wheel and with a very short stroke. The fast passenger locomotive had long horizontal pistons, built for smooth speed. The Shay was ugly, but it could climb like a mountain goat and bounce over tracks that would have derailed an ordinary locomotive in a quarter-mile.

The logs were hoisted onto the cars by a steam-driven "jammer." The pike pole men were now replaced by lumberjacks with claw-like "peaveys." They stood on the cars, while the jammer dangled a ton of logs above them, often erratically. It was their job, with the peavey, to get the swinging log into its proper place on the car. Teamwork, balance, leverage. Brute strength was incidental. If the log swung wildly, or the cable slipped on the jammer, only sharp eyes, speed, and skill could save the lumberjack from painful and often crippling injuries.

It would be pleasant to add that these remarkable men, certainly among the most skilled of all skilled workmen engaged in the most dangerous kind of work, were well paid and well cared for by the companies for whom they worked. They were not.

Though wages varied, all were poor in relation to the skill and danger involved in the work. The lumberjack worked a ten-hour day, and he walked to and from the cutting area, even in below-zero weather. He was cramped into bunkhouses, forty or more to a unit. The bunks were wooden bottomed, covered with a thin layer of straw. Two men slept in a single bunk, six feet in width.

The district forester in Missoula remarked in 1917, "They have been treated not quite as good as work horses, for usually there was more ventilation in the barns than in the bunkhouses."

The Montana Board of Health grew concerned and reported in 1917, "Employers . . . pay little attention to the comfort of employees and to sanitary conditions in the camps."

In the winter, the lumberjacks wore woolen clothing. Wool, when wet, dries slowly and smells mightily. Yet the camps provided no drying rooms. The bunkhouses stank from a mixture of smells compounded from wet wool, sweat (shower facilities were almost non-existent), tobacco (mostly of the chewing variety), kerosene, and stale food.

The men ate in mess halls. "The rule of silence" prevailed. No talk, just eat. The food was heavily laden with saltpeter. Vegetables were rare and, when served, had been cooked to mush. The staple was salt pork and saltpetered beef.

All tools, axes, saws, and other equipment had to be sharpened on the lumberjack's own time. On his "time off," where was he to go? He was usually miles from the nearest town. It is small wonder that when, on rare occasions, he did get to town, he got roaring drunk and, often, a bit obstreperous.

The bigger camps had company stores. The men were often paid, in part, in "script," because many stores accepted only that. Prices were high, but often the men could buy nowhere else. It was good business for the company. When company stores were beginning to be widely criticized (after 1915), the companies responded that these stores were merely "service institutions for the men."

Discontent among the lumberjacks had been simmering since the turn of the century. In August 1917, it exploded into the most widespread strike in the history of the industry. It started in Eureka, Montana, and swiftly spread all over the Pacific Northwest. The companies asserted that the strike was the direct result of the agitation of The Industrial Workers of the World (IWW). Commonly called "Wobblies," the IWWs were, indeed, Marxist oriented and violence prone. It was true that they were agitating in the woods camps. But whereas the companies asserted that there were between 3,500 and 4,000 "Wobblies" involved, subsequent research places the figure at about 500.

If, indeed, this was a "Marxist" strike, consider the demands of the lumberjacks: increase of wages, no work on holidays and Sundays, better sanitation, no more than twelve loggers to a bunkhouse, single bunks with springs, shower baths and drying rooms, adequate lighting, and an eight-hour day.

Happily (as did *not* happen in the concurrent miner's strike) the Montana Lumberman's Association, led by the Anaconda Company, convened a marathon meeting at Missoula. The Anaconda Company and Northern Pacific Railroad, as the biggest employers, urged the granting of the demands. Essentially all of the demands were granted, and the strike ended.

Since the Anaconda Company was plagued by violent strikes in its mines from 1917 to 1946, while relative peace reigned in the woods camps, it is a pity that their wisdom in dealing with the lumberjacks was never matched in their dealings with the miners.

II

Technology in the lumber industry developed unevenly, sometimes demonstrating startling ingenuity and sometimes a startling lack of it.

The first sawmill in Montana was built by Father Ravalli at the mission at Stevensville in 1845. It featured four wagon wheels, a belt, a horse, and a saw blade.

It was the discovery of gold that set off a vast demand for lumber in 1862. Mills sprang up like proverbial mushrooms. Many were magnificently "rube-goldbergish." The earliest were water powered, but steam came quickly. It would be fruitless to chronicle the types and the places. By 1864, these "contraptions" were everywhere. They produced, for the most part, only two grades of lumber: (1) sluice and flume and (2) building lumber. The price? About $140 per thousand for sluice and flume, and $125 per thousand for building lumber. All lumber was green, and there were no drying kilns. Who could wait? The first planer was installed by A. M. Holter in Helena in 1864. But planers were rare for many years. After all, it cost an additional $20 per thousand for planed lumber.

The real explosion in mills and lumbering, however, dates to the early 1880s. Miners could not "deep mine" or "quartz mine" without stulls, beams, and braces; nor could they build or operate stamp or crusher mills without vast quantities of all types of lumber. Above all, they could not build or operate copper smelters.

Precisely at the same time that underground mining created a voracious appetite for lumber, the railroads were completed through Montana. Railroads required 3,000 ties per mile of rail, and all trestles and bridges were made of lumber.

Lest the enormity of what was then occurring escape us, consider that by 1884 sawmills west of the Divide were supplying the four-year-old Anaconda Company with 300,000 cords of wood for smelter fuel alone—and this at five dollars per cord. Very shortly, the company's mines were using 40,000 feet of timber *per day.* Only one mine and one smelter!

(Though it may seem to have no place in this section of this book, let us pause to note that all of this timber was being cut from the public domain in blatant contravention of federal law. This led not only to veritable warfare between mining magnates in Montana, a critical factor in the famous "War of the Copper Kings," but it also led to political warfare between Montanans and the federal government. *Mirabile dictu,* and for better or worse, Montanans won.)

From 1884 onward, the logging industry was huge, its technology was advanced, its importance to Montana almost incalculable. It is merely a commentary on the telescoping of time and technology that we must remind ourselves again that late into the 1930s the horse was still the basic power unit in the industry.

Yet technology was woefully slow to develop in the care and feeding of the forest resources themselves. We were profligate. We did not reseed or replant. Most notably, we made no effort to control fires.

It took an immense and awesome fire to wake us up. In 1910, conditions were ripe for tragedy. The forests were tinder dry. The fire season began early. By July 15, 3,000 men were fighting about ninety fires. Then, on August 20, a great wind arose, and the separate fires, in effect, joined—and moved eastward at a rate of about seventy miles per hour. President Taft called upon the regular Army—which was helpless.

The huge fire burned up 3 million acres of virgin timber; it killed eighty-five people; it burned much of Wallace, Idaho, and Taft, Montana; its estimated cost was $695 million (in 1910 dollars and in timber values alone). Many thousands of animals perished; great watersheds dried up for years. Only the snows of fall finally extinguished the fire.

The Great Fire of 1910 is important because (to oversimplify a bit) it led to a great build up of appropriation and fire-control activities of the then newly organized United States Forest Service; it led to the lookout system, much of which is still extant, and, later, to air patrol and smoke jumpers; it led to the creation of private "Forest Protective Associations;" it led, above all, to a profoundly changed attitude toward the care of our forest resources. It had more than a ripple effect—it had a wave effect. Indeed, it may not be hyperbolic to say that forest management as we conceive of it today has at least one deep root buried in the ashes of that holocaust.

To everything, there is, indeed, a season. In a sense, we have come full circle, with forest scientists now saying that some fire is essential to forest rebirth and good health. And, they say, in some areas, fires should either be set—or should be allowed to burn. Historians are in no position to argue that point. We can only assert that the Great Fire of 1910 gave an essential kind of impetus to modern forest management all over America.

"Chokered and ready." Winter log sledding in buffalo coats. Western Montana, ca. 1885. *Courtesy William E. Farr.*

Extensive flume system transporting logs from French Gulch across the Continental Divide, over the mountains to valley floor and railhead, for shipment to Butte and Anaconda. *Courtesy United States Forest Service, Region One Archives.*

Allen Company cutting stulls and cordwood in French Gulch and Mill Creek area to fuel smelters in Butte and Anaconda. Deer Lodge County, ca. 1900. *Courtesy University of Montana Archives.*

Transferring logs from flume to railroad cars on the way to Butte and Anaconda, 1906. *Courtesy University of Montana Archives.*

Terminus of flume system. Deer Lodge valley, 1906. *Courtesy United States Forest Service, Region One Archives.*

Log wagon with wooden wheels used at Knudsen's Camp. Marion, Montana, July 18, 1904. *Courtesy United States Forest Service, Region One Archives.*

Early sawmill in Gallatin Valley, wooden wheels and wooden sleds. This mill cut an average of 13,000 feet per day. July, 1902. *Courtesy United States Forest Service, Region One Archives.*

Small steam-tractor operated sawmill cutting logs, ca. 1915. *Courtesy United States Forest Service.*

"From logging camp to stumptown." Lumberjacks navigating the Whitefish River, Whitefish, Montana, ca. 1910. *Courtesy Montana Historical Society.*

Logging Ponderosa pine in the Bitterroot Valley, ca. 1900. *Courtesy Henry Grant.*

Winter logging camp near Libby, Montana, ca. 1900. *Courtesy William E. Farr.*

Allen Lumber Company's operation in French Gulch, Montana, with camp, store, and post office, 1906. *Courtesy University of Montana Archives.*

Inside the company store — conversation, company, and commodities. French Gulch, Montana. *Courtesy University of Montana Archives.*

Allen Company Store, false front, and mules. French Gulch, Montana. *Courtesy University of Montana Archives.*

"Harnessed and ready for the day's work." Morning in French Gulch, 1906. *Courtesy University of Montana Archives.*

Baking bread at Christmas for the logging camp celebration. French Gulch, Montana. *Courtesy University of Montana Archives.*

Sawing stulls (shaft supports) for the Butte mines, ca. 1905. *Courtesy University of Montana Archives.*

Detail of Blackfoot River jam, 1908.
Courtesy University of Montana Archives.

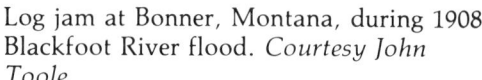

Log jam at Bonner, Montana, during 1908 Blackfoot River flood. *Courtesy John Toole.*

Blasting log jam on Owl Creek to release water for spring drive. Near Seeley Lake, Montana, ca. 1906. *Courtesy John Toole.*

Bateau boat crossing Big Blackfoot River, 1909. *Courtesy Dengler Collection, University of Montana Archives.*

Peavey men on log drive. Blackfoot River, ca. 1908. *Courtesy Dengler Collection, University of Montana Archives.*

Lumberjacks in front of chinked log bunkhouse with tools of trade. Winter camp in French Gulch, Montana, 1906. *Courtesy University of Montana Archives.*

Camp kitchen and dining room at headquarters on Arkansas Creek. Potomac, Montana, 1912. *Courtesy University of Montana Archives.*

Camp No. 2 Cookhouse. Seeley Lake, Montana, 1908. *Courtesy United States Department of Agriculture.*

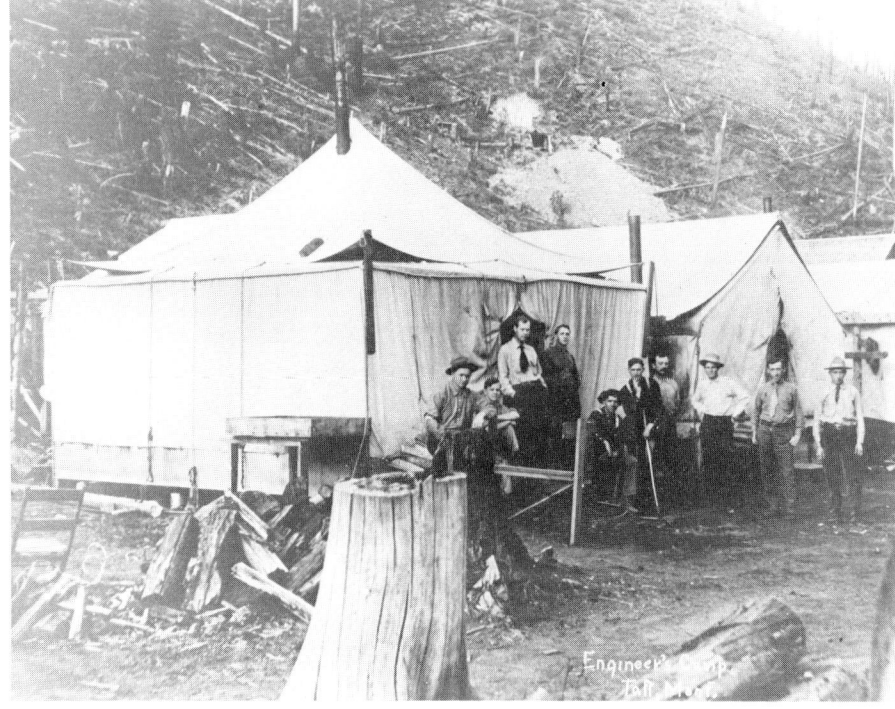

Increased United States Forest Service activity, Engineer's camp at Taft, Montana, 1911. *Courtesy University of Montana Archives.*

The 1910 Fire and its aftermath. Montana-Idaho border, 1910. *Courtesy United States Forest Service, Region One Archives.*

Peavey men. Babb, Montana, ca. 1910. *Courtesy Sherburne Collection.*

Lumberjacks around sled bringing dinner to field. *Courtesy University of Montana Archives.*

Mill workers at Eureka Lumber Company. Eureka, Montana, 1917. *Courtesy University of Montana Archives.*

"Labor unrest among mill workers and lumbermen." Eureka, Montana, 1909. *Courtesy Lincoln County Library.*

FELLOW WORKINGMEN!

NOTICE!

ROTTEN EGGS

Eureka, June 1909

Don't Forget the Rotten Egg Deal!

They rotten egged our speakers on the street. Don't forget it! Now they want you to vote for Eureka for the County Seat.

NOW IS YOUR CHANCE!

Don't forget the Rotten Eggs! Get Even! Don't vote for Eureka for the County Seat!

The Committee of the Industrial Workers of the World.

Left: Corduroy tote road along a gravity chute. Swan Valley, ca. 1900. *Courtesy University of Montana Archives. Above:* Horses trailing logs in chute to Mill pond. ACM camp at Greenough, Montana, 1927. *Courtesy University of Montana Archives.*

"Sand Monkey at his furnace." Heating sand to retard log speed in chutes. Winter, Greenough, Montana, 1925. *Courtesy University of Montana Archives.*

Out of the woods by chute. Mechanical tractor at Greenough, Montana, 1927. *Courtesy University of Montana Archives.*

Left: Steep Chutes on Calahan Creek, Kootenai National Forest, 1926. *Courtesy United States Forest Service, Region One Archives.* *Above:* "Doping" chutes with "holy oil" in the summertime to reduce log friction in the wooden chutes. *K. D. Swan, photographer. Courtesy United States Forest Service, Region One Archives.*

Heading for the mill with Shea locomotive. Northwestern Montana. *Courtesy United States Forest Service, Region One Archives.*

Harry Dengler, camp clerk, Potomac, 1912. *Courtesy University of Montana Archives.*

Out of the woods by flume. Rolling logs into flume, Skookum Creek Sale, Lolo National Forest, 1924. *Courtesy United States Forest Service, Region One Archives.*

Out of the woods by sleigh. Sleigh load of logs at Henry Good Camp, Kalispell Region, 1920. This load of larch logs, eighteen feet long, scaled at 18,030 feet. *Courtesy United States Forest Service, Region One Archives.*

"Stagged pants and horse power." Skidding down steep slope, 1932. *Courtesy United States Forest Service, Region One Archives.*

Bucking logs with cross-cut saws at skidway, Greenough, Montana, 1927. *Courtesy University of Montana Archives.*

Landing, Callahan Creek Sale, 1926. *Courtesy United States Forest Service, Region One Archives.*

Library car for company loggers. Anaconda Copper Mining Company logging operation on Blackfoot River, ca. 1918. *Courtesy University of Montana Archives.*

Neils Brothers Mill, Libby, 1936. *K. D. Swan, photographer. Courtesy United States Forest Service, Region One Archives.*

The destruction of fire and blow-down. Forest fires of 1910. *Courtesy United States Forest Service, Region One Archives.*

Cowboys and Sheepmen

I

It is odd that the cowboy has become the source and substance of an unending American morality play: good versus evil; the lone moralist against the immoral group; the self-sufficient, wise, and courageous loner against all the organized amoral forces besetting our pristine land—and our sense of American virtue.

He was alone, lean, two-gunned, quick, taciturn, but fundamentally gentle. He was utterly self-sufficient—horse, saddle, all his goods and needs in a small roll behind the cantle. On the rare occasions when he met a woman, he was quietly courtly but mysterious. When he met a bad man, and thus came face to face with something rotten, he was patient and silent in the face of insult until, when true righteousness could bear no more, the flash of his hands and the blaze of his guns put evil forever to rest in the dark heap of his enemy upon the ground. Then he rode slowly off, still mysterious, still silent, into a setting sun—always westward.

This set scene is as invariable as tragedy was to the Greeks. And as with the Greeks, the players in the foreground are set off by the chorus in the background, except, perhaps, less obviously.

If the Greek chorus chanted the inevitable, to remind the audience of what had to come, the American audience has never needed a reminder. The chorus was the great, stark, lonely land of which the lone cowboy was an integral part—and into that harmony, the evil group moved in contravention of the land and all virtues.

So it has been with pulp magazines for many years. So it has been in motion pictures and novels innumerable. So it has been, beyond the point of tedium, with television. The play has been well done a dozen times and poorly done several thousand times. But always, it is the play.

There are several startling things about this phenomenon. The first is that there has been such an enormous feast on so little food; the second is that the open-range cowboy operated for so short a time, and yet his presumed activities have fed drama for what seems an eternity; the third is that in the play or the myth, the real cowboy and his very real courage and life style have been obfuscated by romantic stereotypes. Not so the contemporary sheepman. While the cowboy rocketed to romantic heights, the sheepherder, also a stockman and often a cowman temporarily transformed by the realities of the market place, remained a simple, docile herdsman—without a myth, without a following.

In trying to reclaim the real men and the real era, in trying to reveal their stature, we must distinguish between the "open-range" cowboy and the cowboy who worked for a big outfit on the side after he had squatted, homesteaded, or bought railroad land which he owned in fee simple and fenced.

The "open-range" rancher did not "own" the land upon which he grazed his vast herds. He *used* the public domain, for which he paid nothing. That was not illegal. It was simply that a vast, rolling grassland was empty and seemingly limitless in extent. It was empty because the buffalo had been killed off (some 30,000,000 of them, obviously an estimate, had grazed on the Great Plains until the early 1870s. By 1884, almost all of them had been slaughtered). The slaughter of the buffalo left the huge area to herds of antelope, deer, elk, and wolves. But these creatures were, in effect, lost and almost invisible in the tall, high-protein native grass.

Montana's open range was the most desirable on the Great Plains. The range was lower in altitude than the central plains—Wyoming and Colorado; it was richer in soil and water than the southern plains (Texas, New Mexico, and Oklahoma). The grass of eastern Montana put "hard" weight on cattle faster than any other grass in any other area of the American West.

Thus it was that great herds of cattle were driven upon it from about 1875 to 1886. Note the dates, because this is the period of the open range and the open-range cowboy—*about* eleven years.

Who were these open-range cowboys, from whence did they come, what did they do, and how long did they stay? As to who they were, they were "drovers"—that is, they came into Montana driving large herds of longhorn cattle from Texas, southern California, Oklahoma, and, surprisingly, from Oregon. And perhaps even more surprisingly, from *western* Montana.

Why these long drives? Because by 1875, the population in Oregon country had stabilized, and there was a surplus of beef. The result was a series of great cattle drives from *west* to *east,* almost entirely ignored by historians.

Why the great drives northward from Texas, Oklahoma, and southern California? Because in the early '70s, that region was stricken by drought and because the ranges had simply filled up and overgrazing was pandemic. Why the drives from the lush valleys of western Montana? Because the western valley herds, grown and bred to feed the miners, had simply grown too large. As the placer-gold frontier of the 1860s and early 1870s petered out, the mountain-valley ranchers found themselves with overgrazed pastures and a dwindling market. They also recognized that the railroad, probing westward (rails-end was then in North Dakota), represented a quick route to potential market for middle-western and eastern beef consumers.

So, somewhat simplistically, those were the reasons for the great cattle drives into Montana from the South and the West, and that is why, for about a decade, the vast plains of eastern Montana were the home and the realm of the open-range cowboy.

Who was he? Well, almost anyone who could ride a horse, had no home ties, would work dirt cheap, eat poor food, suffer great danger, and endure constant discomfort and interminable hours. He came from the South, East, or West. Racially, he was anybody and everybody—most assuredly including Blacks. He was apt to be a Civil War veteran, particularly southern. He was very often Mexican because of the Texas drives. He was almost always young, because only a young man could take the physical beating.

In Montana, what was the "home" ranch like after the drives were finished? Well, not like the Ponderosa. If the rancher had filed on any land at all, it was a 160-acre plot on a spring site or a river bank. Beyond that, on what he called "customary range," he ran five thousand to twelve thousand cattle—no fences, no clearly delineated boundaries. The "home ranch" usually consisted of a one- or two-room log house, a corral for horses, a bunkhouse of poles or sod, and perhaps a well.

There were two roundups—the first was in the spring to brand the calves. The spring roundup covered a huge area. Cattle from all ranches in the area were driven to a central place chosen by the roundup captain. Each rancher sent cowboys on a pro rata basis—so many men for so many cattle. They would fan out over a huge countryside and drive the cattle to the central area. Once in the central area, the cowboy had to cut out the calves, rope them, tie them, and brand them. There were no corrals; there were no squeeze chutes; there were no propane-fired branding machines; there were no fences. There was only the cowboy, the rope, the calf, the branding iron, and the branding fire. And there were these factors also: blinding dust, drizzling rain, awesome heat, chilling cold, mud, terrible wind—and food cooked into a gray mush. At night, a blanket, a rattling slicker, and your clothes on, including your boots. There were no "sleeping bags."

So fierce was the demand upon man and beast that the one thing a cowboy could not afford was an exhausted horse. Therein lay danger. Accordingly, the horse remuda, overseen by "wranglers," consisted of roughly eight to ten horses per cowboy. No two or three horses could stand the beating. Oddly enough, the "wranglers" (Charles M. Russell was a wrangler) were low men on the totem pole. They were not sufficiently skilled to ride, rope, throw, tie, and brand. Yet, of course, their function was vital.

If one of the duties of the cowboy was the spring roundup, another was the fall roundup. Here the whole scene was repeated—except that there was no branding. The object was to cut out the "fat cattle" (usually two- or three-year-olds) for the long drive to rail's end. Between roundups, the cowboy's job was to "ride the herd." For this function, his area was usually hundreds of square miles. "Line camps" were rare. He had to carry jerky with him or shoot his own game. What he needed, he had to carry on his horse and pack horse. He was "lost" to civilization for four to five months. His job was to count cattle, and (in the early '80s) to fight off, shoot, or scare off wolves. He had to rope and treat sick cattle as best he could. He had to cope with blistering heat, flash floods, violent temperature changes, snow in July, and drought in August. And all of this, recall, for thirty dollars a month. If he had a "six-shooter" at all, it was for the abundant rattlesnakes. He carried a rifle, usually a .30-caliber, to shoot game.

Why did these men, so highly skilled at their jobs, do what they did for so little pay and at so great a price—in comfort, loneliness, and danger? Who now could really be so presumptuous as to say? But the answer might lie in the fact that the word "freedom" conjures up awesome semantic complexities. The cowboy was not "free." Indeed, he was terribly restricted by the laws of nature. He was hemmed in by hills, by cold, by heat, by rivers, by sickness (there were no doctors), by pay, by blizzards, by distance, and by loneliness. But in a deeper sense, he was, of course, as free as any man has ever been. Because maybe he asked merely this: "I ask nothing of any man. I live or die solely on the basis of my own skill, my own wits, my own knowledge of this malevolent land." That is, indeed, a wondrous kind of freedom. But the myth never really deals with the cost of it—only with the glories. And the myth never tells us that this reckless breed of man plied his trade for only about a decade. And then it was gone—destroying itself, never to return.

II

The open range did not end as of May 2, at 2 P.M., 1887. But it might as well have. Much was lost with it, including the cowboy as we conceive of him today. What happened?

The hard winter of 1886–1887 has been written about to such an extent that it has become a kind of cliche. It was not really the hard winter of 1886–1887 that put an end to the era of the open-range and the cowboy. Nor, indeed, did the cowboy suddenly cease to be a cowboy. It is simply that the man he had been now began to respond to subtle pressures to make him something else. He did not quickly lose what he had been nor quickly become what he was to be.

In the fall of 1886, there were about one million cattle on the eastern Montana ranges. The summer had been terribly dry. The range was grossly overgrazed. The price of cattle was low, so that many cattlemen held over their "fat cattle."

A terrible winter struck. Early on, there was a heavy, wet snow; then a chinook melted the snow over an area of some 50,000 square miles. Then came a series of terrible blizzards which converted the water into a vast sheet of ice; then cold, blizzard, cold again; often 30° or 40° below zero. The cattle died—not by the hundreds or thousands, but by the hundreds of thousands. Record-keeping was poor in those days, and we will never know the real figures. But some "old outfits," such as the DHS, figured their loss at seventy-five percent.

The tragedy was complex—too many cattle, too many weak trail cattle (from Texas, exhausted by the drive), too many cattle for a drought-weakened range, too few cowboys with too little, if any, feed. Essentially, however, the hard winter of 1886–1887 simply represented an abuse of the land. "Hard winters" are, and always have been, a part of the cycle of the Great Plains. It was, in final substance, merely a case of man placing too much pressure on the land for quick profit.

The cattle industry recovered with remarkable speed. The census tells us that. But what it does not tell us is that a "type" was destroyed. A kind of man was destroyed; a kind of freedom was destroyed. And the cowboy began a kind of adaptation and a kind of transition which the myth and the morality play have never recognized.

With rather stunning suddenness, the cowboy became part farmer, raising hay and grain to guard against another catastrophe. Likewise, many a homesteader interested in agriculture found that he could not make it by farming alone, and he turned to cattle. Diversification set in. Market prices channeled not only interest, but practice; cowmen turned to sheep and farming, and homesteaders raised stock. The cowboy became an irrigator, a tractor driver, a primitive mechanic. He became a builder of fences with a narrowed geographical spectrum. There is that song, you know, written by an old-time Montanan, "Don't Fence Me In." But that was nostalgic, because that is precisely what the cowboy did—because he *had* to; he fenced himself in.

This was a painful period of transition when the new mixed with the old and the customary. Transition came, however: it came in methods of fencing, and stacking hay; in wagons, canvas tents, and stores; sheep, automobiles, ferries, and even with women in working chaps. The pressure of change was inescapable and it became shockingly visible to all who looked. The tenacity of the old ways was remarkable. In faces, in places, in clothing, in horse tack and ropes, the characteristics of the past died slowly or not at all. Often they simply took on a newer appearance. And, of course, some things do not change at all. The horse, the remuda, and the wide rivers remained what they had been. How slowly, how painfully, that strangely restricted freedom of open land and open life died.

The myth of the cowboy, however, flourished. His quiet self-sufficiency, his independence, and his courage shaped ideals concerning the West. Whether sheep rancher, wheat rancher, or lowly drugstore cowboy, the cowboy ethos percolated through western society, infusing it with an image few could live. It conquered all in some mysterious fashion—sheepmen for example, lived similar lives, perhaps even more lonely, more nomadic, more independent; and they lived that life longer. But they lacked the myth, and they still do.

Cowboying was never as clean and straight as myth has made it. There was permutation, adaptation, and rapid change. Cows, sheep, and grain were not mutually exclusive—but all came to share the characteristics that had made the myth of the cowboy.

Cowboys on Fallon Roundup in front of Bandwagon Store. Fallon, Montana, ca. 1910. R. C. Morrison, photographer. Courtesy Mrs. Richard Smith.

Trailing cattle on the Fergus Ranch near Lewiston, Montana Territory, ca. 1880. *Courtesy University of Montana Archives.*

"Polled Angus cattle grazing at Spring Coulee near 'Crofts' outside of Benton Township." Fort Benton, Montana Territory, 1885. This is exceptionally early for purebred cattle. *Courtesy Conrad Collection, University of Montana Archives.*

Roundup encampment on the range near Deer Lodge, Montana, ca. 1890s.
Courtesy William E. Farr.

Rope corral. Roundup time near Miles City, ca. 1900. *R. C. Morrison, photographer. Courtesy Mrs. Richard Smith.*

Pushing cattle herd across the Yellowstone River near Miles City, Montana, ca. 1900. Even cowboys wore suspenders and rowed boats. *R. C. Morrison, photographer. Courtesy Mrs. Richard Smith.*

XIT cowboys at dinner. Miles City, Montana, 1904. *Courtesy L. Archdale Collection, University of Montana Archives.*

N-N cowboys adjusting saddles on trail drive. Northwestern Montana, ca. 1890. *Courtesy Montana Historical Society.*

Breaking camp in morning light. Northern Montana, ca. 1900. *Courtesy Sherburne Collection.*

COW BOYS AND SADDLE PONNIES IN CAMP ON THE RANGE.

Left, above: XIT Indian crew near Browning, Montana, on Blackfeet Reservation, ca. 1910. *Courtesy Montana Historical Society. Left, below:* Cowboy "stag" dance near Glendive, Montana. *Courtesy Frontier Gateway Museum. Above:* Ferrying cowboys across the Yellowstone River at Terry, Montana. *E. J. Cameron, photographer. Courtesy J. H. Trafton.*

The Knowlton Store at Terry, Montana, 1904. *E. S. Cameron, photographer. Courtesy J. H. Trafton.*

Ranch house interior. Big Sandy, Montana. *Courtesy Al Lucke.*

Above: Loading bedwagon for CK roundup. Fountain Ranch, Circle, Montana, 1912. *Courtesy Verna Carlson.*
Left: Texas trailhands in Lone Star Saloon listening to early gramaphone. Circle, Montana, 1896. *Courtesy Verna Carlson.*
Right, below: Winter feeding near Miles City, Montana, ca. 1905. *E. S. Cameron, photographer. Courtesy L. Archdale Collection, University of Montana Archives.*
Right, above: Tar paper, green lumber, and tent. Home ranch near Fallon, Montana, ca. 1905. *John L. Breum, photographer. Courtesy J. H. Trafton.*

Left, above: A cowboy's funeral. Glendive, Montana. *Courtesy Montana Historical Society. Left, below:* Asa Kempton and roped coyote. Fallon, Montana, 1902. *E. S. Cameron, photographer. Courtesy L. Archdale Collection, University of Montana Archives. Above:* Cowboy's "bed room" near Glendive, Montana. *Courtesy Frontier Gateway Museum.*

Roundup morning in Havre. PX roundup crew, 1906. *Courtesy Al Lucke.*

Charlie "Dynamite" Hanson's Store, Fallon, Montana, ca. 1906. *E. J. Cameron, photographer. Courtesy J. H. Trafton.*

"Pooling and repping." Cowboy rendezvous in east-central Montana. *Courtesy Montana State University Archives.*

XIT cowboys shopping in Fallon, Montana, ca. 1906. *John Breum, photographer. Courtesy J. H. Trafton.*

Crossing the Missouri River near the Breaks. *Courtesy Al Lucke.*

Sunday afternoon near Terry, Montana.
*E. S. Cameron, photographer. Courtesy
L. Archdale Collection, University of
Montana Archives.*

Point of Rock Hotel and Stage Station,
1895. *Courtesy Thomas B. Brooks.*

Ranch house in north-central Montana, ca. 1900. *Courtesy Al Lucke.*

Death comes to a drifting cowboy inside ranch house. Wolf Point, Montana, ca. 1900. *Courtesy Wolf Point Historical Museum.*

Cook feeding leftovers to out-of-picture horse, 1905. *R. C. Morrison, photographer. Courtesy Mrs. Richard Smith.*

"Cowboys bellying up to the bar." *Courtesy Montana State University Archives.*

Left, above: Sunday picnic. Miles City, Montana, ca. 1905. *R. C. Morrison, photographer. Courtesy Mrs. Richard Smith. Left, below:* Ready for the brand. Fallon, Montana, 1904. *John Breum, photographer. Courtesy J. H. Trafton. Above:* Snubbed and ready; Lord Cameron and crew. Fallon, Montana, 1905. *E. J. Cameron, photographer. Courtesy J. H. Trafton.*

"My front gate," near Dillon, Montana. *Courtesy Montana Historical Society.*

Unusual Hutterite cowboy. Northern Montana. *Courtesy Montana State University Archives.*

Above: Beginnings of Glascow, Montana. *Courtesy University of Montana Archives. Left:* The Graves' spread — a typical eastern Montana ranch north of Glendive, 1896. *Courtesy M. L. Graves.*

After a hard winter, February 1904. *E. S. Cameron, photographer. Courtesy L. Archdale Collection, University of Montana Archives.*

Cowboys amid large herd of cattle on Kohrs ranch near Deer Lodge, 1900. *Courtesy University of Montana Archives.*

Blackfeet cowboys at Browning, Montana, 1903. *Courtesy Sherburne Collection.*

Diversification comes to the range — hay, cattle, sheep. Near Glendive, Montana. *A. S. Foss, photographer. Courtesy M. L. Graves.*

Sheep on the range north of Fallon, Montana, 1905. *E. J. Cameron, photographer. Courtesy J. H. Trafton.*

Jessie and Brownie in their sheepwagon home, 1905. *E. J. Cameron, photographer. Courtesy J. H. Trafton.*

Shearing sheds on one of James W. Gilmore's ranches. Dawson County, Montana Territory, 1885. *Courtesy Frontier Gateway Museum.*

Left, above: Rodeo cowboys at Missoula Stampede. Fairgrounds, Missoula, Montana, 1916. *Courtesy William E. Farr.*
Left, below: Rodeo cowboys on tour during the Depression. *Courtesy Mrs. Rial Carney. Right:* Young Big Sandy cowboys with the accoutrement of their image. *Courtesy Montana Historical Society.*

St. Mary's River and Chief Mountain, near Babb, Montana. *Courtesy Sherburne Collection.*

Reservation Indians in Montana

Sociologists and anthropologists use a word, "acculturation," which lends itself to a variety of interpretations. Essentially, however, "acculturation" describes a process in which an "adaptation" occurs, when two societies with different ethnic, religious, and historical roots encounter each other. Under certain conditions, the result is a kind of blending, melding, or merging—with both societies enriched as an end result.

However, the more disparate the societies, the more difficult the "melding" becomes. If one of the societies is much stronger (numerically, technologically, or militarily), the resultant encounter may be tragic for the weaker society—and in the long run, less salubrious for the stronger society. The latter tends to be blind to the lessons it might learn from the former. It tends to demand that the weaker society conform completely to the mores, ideals, and "way of life" of the stronger.

Essentially, that is what happened to the Montana Indian. When at last he had been confined to reservations; when his economic base had been destroyed; when his religion had been vitiated by the incessant bombardment of Christian missionaries, the situation was ripe for his total absorption into "the mainstream of American life." If there was an Indian theme around the turn of the century, it was the theme of the "vanishing American," the "buffalo nickel," and the "end of the trail." It was pervasive; it was persuasive. All agreed, all harbingers indicated the Indians' complete disappearance as a discrete people. Consequently, legions of dedicated scientists, missionaries, museums, and photographers enrolled in a grand scientific enterprise—the documentation of the vanishing, primitive life of the American Indian. The residue of this prodigious task remains impressive—massive museum collections, which only now are again resurfacing as public interest returns, multi-volumed ethnographical studies, numerous novels and artistic depictions, and most of all, an abiding interest for all Americans in the first American. Registered in the pages of *Sunset Magazine*, reflected in tourism to the West, or in collections of Navajo rugs or Northwest Coast sewing baskets, the Indian "craze" even manifested itself in the *Ladies Home Journal* of 1908 with a feature on how to decorate the Victorian home with an Indian motif.

There was a sense of urgency. Somehow the romantic, aboriginal past had to be seized before it and the American Indian himself disappeared forever, lost either through degradation, disease, and the destructive qualities of his nature *or* lost through the beneficial, but equally destructive, process of acculturation.

Yet a strange thing happened—a thing which statistically, politically, and economically should not have happened. The Indians remained, and still remain, a discrete people—Indian. Located on reservations, since 1900 they have increased steadily in numbers (in Montana alone from 11,343 to 27,130). In spite of high infant mortality rate, suicides, alcoholism, unemployment, illiteracy, poverty, and short life expectancy, Indians prevailed and, indeed, they *have* adapted. An unknown number have "crossed over" through intermarriage. But the hard fact remains that today the Indian people remain Indian—more so than at any time since they were first fenced in, utterly at the mercy of a white government essentially dedicated to the proposition that all Indians should become "white."

It is a commentary on Indian resiliency and toughness that today there is no chance that any American government can ever succeed in making the Indian "white." There is irony in the fact that, in essence, the government in Washington is in retreat. Indian claims on ancestral land, on water rights, on some kind of quasi-sovereignty are clogging federal courts. The Indians, including Indians in Montana, are winning more often than they are losing.

We cannot record in the photographs of this section the tribal history of each of Montana's seven reservations. We can and did select visual examples that were symptomatic of reservation life throughout Montana in the first quarter of this century. These photographs give us a secure, distinct vision of men and women caught in the bewildering crush of change. Often these individuals wanted to record that change and their own personal odyssey themselves—be they Blackfeet, Cheyenne, Crow, or Assinibone. If they didn't record it, then it was done by local, white photographers. Times changed, and Indians, as have all Americans, welcomed that change, celebrating it on film.

So, as we were gathering Indian photographs for this chapter, we had, vaguely, a theme in mind. The Indian people persevered, but they did so on Montana reservations in a manner that was far removed from the "noble savage" so favored by E. S. Curtis, famed photographer of Indians, as he sought to record the vanishing American. Instead, we would show reservation life as it really was after the innocence and romanticism of the pre-war period had worn off, after the Indian had submerged, had disappeared from the popular consciousness. Acculturated too much to be romantic, he was only degraded. And on reservations in Montana, Indian life became more and more bleak—the survival of a woebegone, forgotten, demoralized people. Even the long-pursued goal of "schooling" the Indian, for Indian and white alike, came to appear chimeral in the generalized questioning of the depression years.

There was achievement, there was sadness, in the process of first acculturation; what followed was worse—neglect. The photographs state that plainly and with force. Notice the photographs of the three Blackfeet at Browning, weaving baskets, and remember that there was no basket-weaving tradition in the history of these horse warriors. There is also irony in these images: the Indian float in a Missoula Stampede of 1915 in which the Flathead Indians themselves are in effect celebrating their forceable removal by the U.S. Army from the Bitterroot to the Flathead valley in 1896. It is as if they were dancing on their own graves.

In sorting photographs, we encountered Indian degradation—and we faced crippling insensitivity on the part of those "instructing"—whether in "boarding schools" or at fairs and agricultural exhibits. But we also found more compelling themes. At first, the themes were subliminal. We resisted them. After all, were these not a beaten and degraded people, lost in the complex maze of modern American life that rendered them "children" or "wards"? Could we really show them any other way? We scrutinized the growing pile of photographs more closely. Yes. The answer was compelling:

we could not avoid the more abiding themes—pride and work.

Again and again, white photographers took pictures of Indians *working.* That activity of the Indian impressed them, and it was that activity they presented in their photographs when they documented the life of their Indian contemporaries. To be sure, working was a white preoccupation, a sign of successful acculturation. Just as sure, however, was the clear necessity for Indians to work. Neither the Bureau of Indian Affairs nor its predecessors ever really supplied the reservation Indian with sufficient "dole" to keep them above an abysmal poverty level. Often the "dole" or "ration" was insufficient to sustain life. Equally often, the natural resources on many reservations were inadequate to make the area economically viable. There was then poverty, but it was ameliorated on the reservation, as elsewhere, by working.

If the Indian was only squatting in his hovel waiting for the "allotment," why are the Crows out threshing in the heat of that August day? What are the Casey Scouts near Fort Keogh doing in that awesomely bitter cold? What are the Blackfeet lumberjacks doing with their "snow-blind" glasses, their crosscut saws and axes? Who is operating the sawmill on the Fort Belknap Reservation?

So, on all the reservations in Montana, there they are: Indians herding cattle, herding sheep, laboring on irrigation projects, logging, planting, plowing, harvesting, mining, selling buffalo horns, or dancing for Great Northern tourists—doing anything and everything they could *do* on the sparse land "given" them by the government. And when they could not employ themselves on the reservation, they went off it, traveling individually and in groups, to the Okanogon valley in Washington, to Yakima to pick fruit, to prune, to top sugar beets near Sidney, Montana, and to be migratory labor.

Indians adapted; they labored, and they survived. Study the photograph of Mad Plume and his family. He is obviously a sheepman. But what is far more inescapable is that Mad Plume's family is strong, close, and it is *Indian.* Here, as elsewhere, there is "adaptation," but there is also authority and self-awareness. And there is cohesiveness—the bond of kin-relation which secured for so many, through mutual assistance and mutual dependence, a sense of strength and endurance.

It is not our intent in this chapter to gloss over the grim facts of reservation life nor to portray Indian life in Montana as a series of "pow-wows." The facts of reservation life were grim, and grim they remain. Photographers documented that aspect of Indian life all too well. Those segments of life are not to be ignored. But this proposition is worth some thought: toughness, spirit, dignity, and adaptability are not qualities which some peoples have and others do not. There are few more empirical examples of that fact than the long refusal of Indians to cease being Indian.

Left: Blackfeet Indians selling buffalo horns to tourists. Northern Montana, ca. 1890. *Courtesy Public Archives of Canada.*
Right: "Crow brave holding mirror as he prepares for the dance." Hardin, Montana, ca. 1890. *Fred Miller, photographer. Courtesy Hulda Fields.*

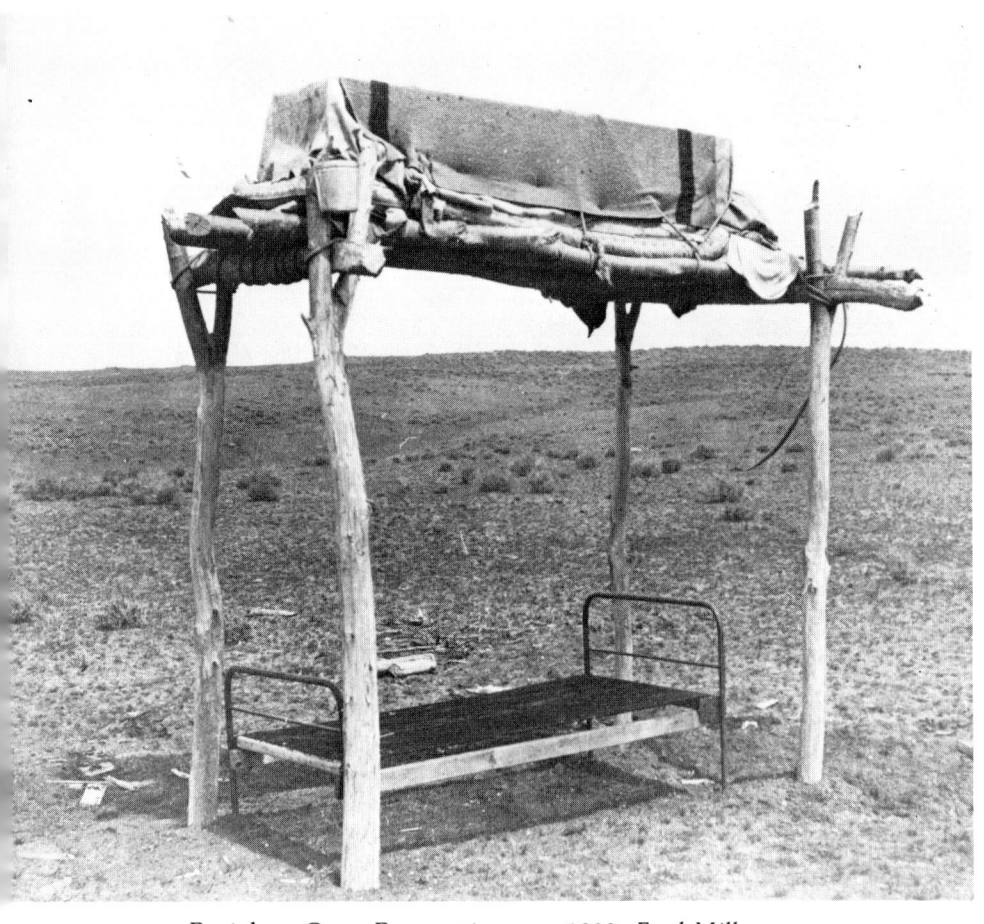

Burial on Crow Reservation, ca. 1890. *Fred Miller, photographer. Courtesy Hulda Fields.*

White Swan, Crow scout for General Custer. *D. H. Coffeen Collection. Courtesy Doug Allard.*

Interior of Northern Cheyenne tepee. *D. H. Coffeen Collection. Courtesy Doug Allard.*

Left: "Allotment Day." Flathead Reservation, ca. 1900. *Courtesy William E. Farr. Left, below:* "Women waiting to receive government rations." Ration Day, Lame Deer, Montana, 1904-1914. *Courtesy University of Montana Archives.*

Interior of house with stove, dishes, and a sack of flour from the Crow Agency Flour Mill. Crow Agency, Montana. *D. H. Coffeen Collection. Courtesy Doug Allard.*

Northern Cheyenne preparing for sweat bath. Lame Deer, Montana, ca. 1910. *Courtesy University of Montana Archives.*

Left, above: "The Casey Scouts approaching Fort Keogh on return from Pine Ridge and the Sioux trouble. And without their commander who was killed by Brule Sioux, Plenty Horses. January 7, 1891." *Courtesy Montana Historical Society. Left, below:* Indian police on the Fort Peck Reservation, 1915. *Courtesy Eastern Montana College Library. Right:* the clash of cultures — "Travois, tracks, and town." *Courtesy William E. Farr.*

Well-equipped, well-suited Frank Wheeler. Assiniboine, Fort Peck Reservation. *Courtesy Montana Historical Society.*

"J. H. Sherburne. U.S. Licensed Trader." Blackfeet Indian Reservation, Browning, Montana, 1908. *J. H. Sherburne, photographer. Courtesy Sherburne Collection.*

Above: "The ceremonial trappings of two cultures." Catholic bishop with Flathead elders. St. Ignatius, Montana, 1910. *Courtesy William E. Farr.* *Left:* "Issuing Supplies." *Courtesy Tim Gordon.*

Slaughtering beef. Allotment Day, Northern Cheyenne Reservation. *Courtesy Eastern Montana College Library.*

Holy Family Mission Band. Blackfeet Reservation, ca. 1910. *Courtesy Glacier Studio.*

Flathead couple with dog, 1910. *Courtesy William E. Farr.*

Assiniboine cowboys on the northern plains, Fort Belknap. *Courtesy Montana Historical Society.*

"All women and no saddles." First horse race at first Crow Fair. *Fred Miller, photographer. Courtesy Hulda Fields.*

Crow cowboys with the remuda. Roundup morning, 1907. *Courtesy University of Montana Archives.*

In the agency slaughterhouse. Blackfeet Reservation, Browning, Montana, ca. 1912. *Courtesy Sherburne Collection.*

Instruction on farming techniques. County extension agent at mid-winter fair, Browning, Montana. *Courtesy Montana Historical Society.*

Family portrait. Flathead Reservation. *Courtesy F. Benson.*

Proud father and daughter. Crow Agency, Montana. *D. H. Coffeen Collection. Courtesy Doug Allard.*

Family portrait. Flathead Reservation. *Courtesy F. Benson.*

St. Ignatius, Montana, 1900. *Edward Boos, photographer. Courtesy University of Montana Archives.*

Pryor Indian Boarding School. Pryor, Montana. *Fred Miller, photographer. Courtesy Hulda Fields.*

Willow Creek Indian Boarding School, Christmas, 1907. Cut Bank, Montana. *Courtesy Sherburne Collection.*

Dining room, Willow Creek School. *Courtesy Sherburne Collection.*

Learning to bake bread. Willow Creek School, 1907. *Courtesy Sherburne Collection.*

"Sewing Classes." Cut Bank Indian School. *Courtesy Sherburne Collection.*

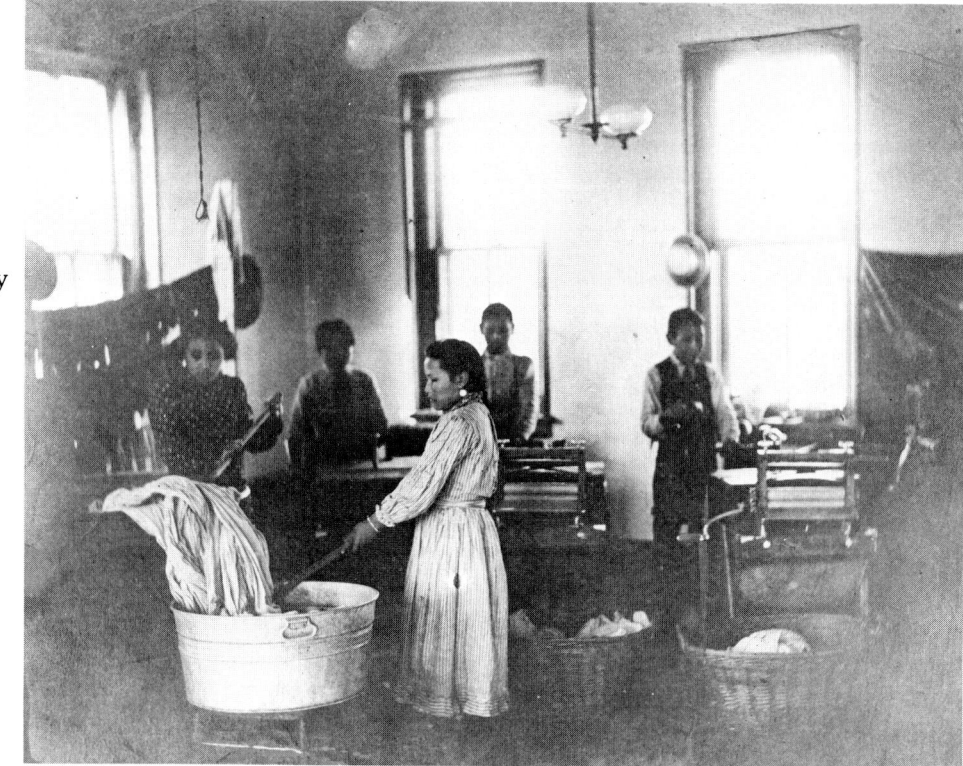

"Learning to wash clothing." Crow Agency School, 1915. *Fred Miller, photographer. Courtesy Hulda Fields.*

Crow Indian girls at boarding school with "Crow" snowman. Lame Deer, Montana, ca. 1918. *Courtesy University of Montana Archives.*

Right: Crow Indians harvesting with team. *Courtesy Montana Historical Society. Below:* Logging operations during winter 1916. Crow Agency, Montana. *D. H. Coffeen Collection. Courtesy Doug Allard.*

"Flathead Dandy." 1920.
Courtesy Montana Historical Society.

Government work and enrichment programs on the Blackfeet Reservation, Browning, Montana. *Courtesy Fred DesRosier.*

Government work, Blackfeet Reservation, Browning, Montana. *Courtesy Fred DesRosier.*

Left: "Flint Family." Heart Butte Blackfeet Reservation, Montana. *Courtesy Fred DesRosier. Below:* Indian teamsters at work on project, United States Reclamation Service. Babb, Montana, ca. 1909. *Courtesy Sherburne Collection.*

Opposite, above: "Government sawmill in Peoples Creek Canyon." Fort Belknap, Montana. *Courtesy Montana Historical Society. Opposite, below:* "Waiting for Tourists," Blackfeet encampment in front of Glacier Park Hotel. East Glacier Park, Montana, ca. 1925. *Courtesy Fred DesRosier.*

Flathead float depicting removal from Bitterroot Valley. Missoula Stampede, Missoula, Montana, 1916. *Courtesy John E. Fox.*

Blackfeet loggers at Browning, Montana. *Courtesy Fred DesRosier.*

Crow women in a game of chance, ca. 1920. *Fred Miller, photographer. Courtesy Hulda Fields.*

The automobile comes to the Reservation. *Forsythe, photographer. Courtesy University of Montana Archives.*

Mad Plume and his family. Blackfeet Reservation, 1925. *Courtesy Fred DesRosier.*

Blackfeet Indian boys. *Courtesy Montana State University Archives.*

Above All, They Made Homes

The successive waves of work-oriented intruders into Montana brought with themselves strong homemaking instincts and considerable baggage, cultural and otherwise. Perhaps the first waves only remembered homes left, but succeeding ones were determined not only to make their fortunes on the opening frontier, but to make their homes there as well. What was it that made a home, what did it include, and how did it import a sense of constancy? However defined, one thing was certain—families were necessary, women and children requisite, and while it is overly simplistic to say that it was the women who brought homes and culture to the lonely, raw country, they certainly meant that settlement and civilization had arrived.

Men and women simply insisted that what they had left behind would be duplicated in the new land. It was not that they had escaped old homes and had gladly abandoned old patterns forever; rather they wanted to build new ones with greater opportunities to expand economic and personal horizons. Moreover, in Montana there seemed to be such a void, so few templates with which to shape a future life. The alternative was to bring the structure and the sustaining patterns with them. Perhaps too much had to be imported into Montana at first, for not everything fit or was capable of adoption and later had to be discarded. Still, at first there came two-storied Wisconsin farm houses, Iowa silos, European round barns, and Scandinavian steepled churches. Celebrations and culture, too, were imported, along with the ethnic mix of Frenchmen, Scots, Irish, German-Russians, and English. And later, industrial mining added to the variety—Chinese, Finns, Italians, Poles, and Czechs. The Old World and eastern America, be it filtered through North Dakota or upstate New York, were transferred to the empty plains and mountains of Montana to be perpetuated.

To work, to establish homes, men and women came as families, and they came to stay. Above all, to stay. This determination to stay, to marry, to settle, and to duplicate whatever they had left manifested itself in a bewildering variety of ways. It is easy to confuse symbols with substance. There are, for instance, accounts of pianos being ordered at great cost from the East, of then after many months of waiting and letters of inquiry, being picked up at some distant, desolate depot. The way home included hauling, ferrying, heaving the piano across the Yellowstone or Missouri, only then to be sledded to a wintry home and to find that the door on the new house was too small. Was this incredible effort and labor just to satisfy some yearning for lost amenities? Was this insistence on things cultural some consequence of nostalgia? No, the motivation was rather a tough determination to assert permanence by establishing homes just like those they had left, those they had grown up with. They did it to convince themselves and others that what they were doing was of value and that it was permanent. "We'll stick, we'll win," was a slogan and an assertion scribbled out in the 1920s as drought, crickets, and dust pushed families out of Montana, but it also expressed an attitude long prevalent in this state. As cultural transplants, the newcomers brought their past with them, and it gave them a semblance of stability in the novelty and flux of Montana.

Fiction and the media have created a myth that has veneered an earlier reality—that in the mining camps, the lumbering towns, and out on the ranches, the furniture was hand-hewn, homemade, and crude. In fact, this was rarely true. Some years ago a remarkable woman, Caroline Mcgill, M.D., decided to collect furniture representative of the period from 1870 to 1900. The Mcgill collection astounded the mythologists. The furniture was solid mahogany, inlaid cherry, polished curly maple, and oak. It was crafted—*finely* crafted—and, indeed, though it was hauled, portaged, pulled, and lifted across the dry plains and borne high into the mountains on wagons or sleds, it was handled as the most precious of cargo. It almost always arrived. No one counted the cost. Sometimes it arrived "distressed," with an unavoidable scratch or its finish marred, but it arrived and was given an honored place in the parlor or bedroom of the home.

There were mirrors. There was porcelain and bone china, silver and pewter, leaded tiffany lamp shades, and crystal. There were books of Shakespeare, Byron, and Burns, of theology, Homer, and Virgil. A wife on the frontier reminisced: "So eager were we to keep in touch with civilization that even when we could not afford a shotgun and ammunition to kill rabbits, we subscribed to newspapers and periodicals and bought books."

In all houses, the less affluent as well as the more prosperous, stringent efforts were made to proclaim permanence and self-improvement. Families, men and women, were not content to be less "genteel" than they had been before. They made few compromises with the rawness, the distance, or the novelty of Montana. Their demands gave rise to mail-order catalogs, Grand Rapids furniture, and the traveling salesman. There is a certain irony in the fact that presently, folk art collectors and antique collectors obsessively collect the handmade and the hand-hewn, calling them "primitives." The fact is that the "folk" were getting away from the primitive as fast as they could. To them it meant transience, and they did not intend to be transients. As quickly as they could, they moved out of the sod house and the tar-paper claiming shack into a frame house, preferably something two-story and with a fireplace. As quickly as they could, they plumbed, planted flowers, and wallpapered the parlor. The trappings of home were the trappings of a cherished culture that needed to be nurtured if it was to become permanent.

Western historians sometimes dwell on the meaning behind the central buildings in the western towns of America—the bank, the saloon, the church, the livery stable, and later the grain elevator. All were necessary, meaningful, solid institutions. Yet, in many respects, the building most central to the community was the schoolhouse—often brick and always as permanent as the community it served. Next to the church and the school in importance was the opera house. Often that opera house had been carefully designed and meticulously constructed to achieve acoustical delights. The gingerbread facing, the elaborate scrolls and newel posts, and the heavy brocade did not indicate pretension, it was cultivation, self-improvement, and gentility. Nor was it built for local talent alone; its stage and orchestra pit housed companies of touring professionals. Though it was indeed an affair of moment, the citizens of Butte, Montana, were hardly "starry-eyed" when Julia Dean Hayne Cooper appeared in *Griseldis* in 1876 at Loeber's Opera House. They turned out in force a week later to hear Captain R. H. Mason lecture on "The Conquest of Mexico." The most popular touring companies of all, however, were the Shakespearean ones. Whether at Philipsburg or St. Ignatius, the opera house or its equivalent retained its lure for a long span of time. In Red Lodge, the Finnish Brotherhood Hall staged play after play, in Finnish and in English, with the costumes coming from Denver, Colorado, at considerable cost. "Kaiser Bill" productions swept through the communities of the "Highline" as war and American patriotism demanded conviction and commitment.

The American concept of "education for all" was Jeffersonian—it was revolutionary, it was anti-class and anti-caste, and it became for all an article of faith. So where the home was, there also was the school—with a school teacher, a bell, perhaps a "facility," and a supporting community. Like the home, public education needed accoutrements. The distance between ideal and reality was, of course, great if you lived in Sumatra or Ingomar, Greenbench or Rexford. Whatever its limitations, however, the one-room school attempted to bridge a cultural gap and an educational lag.

Reading secondary accounts of Montana's early towns on both sides of the mountains, one gets the impression of unrelieved violence—of vigilantes, of shootings, and of hangings—and violence there certainly was. That is particularly true when reading about mining camps, cow towns, railroad terminals, and roaring Butte. But the diaries, letters, newspapers, and *photographs* are strangely devoid of this "popular" view of things. In the pages of the Virginia City *Montana Post*, the Great Falls *Leader*, or the Helena *Radiator*, one reads of literary societies, advertisements for music lessons, language lessons, lectures, church news, club invitations, travel, and just plain gossip.

J. K. Miller, a teenager in Virginia City in 1864, confided practically everything he saw and felt to his diary. At seventeen, he was taking French lessons, enjoying the Virginia City Social Club, and reading with the literary association when he was not squiring "pretty young ladies." He did not like boxing. In reference to one fight, he wrote that it was attended by "a very rough looking crowd" and a very small percentage of "gents."

These concerns continued to have a remarkable vitality in Bear Creek, Brockway, and Ennis as parents sacrificed to establish schools, pay for music lessons, buy books, and create public libraries to lend to those who could not afford to buy books.

Life was more slowly paced then, simpler and punctuated more often by ceremony and celebration in the home, the school, and the community. The miner, slogging in muck and darkness, was filthy, rough, profane, and belligerent for six days a week. On Sunday, however, he was a different man. Scrubbed clean, dressed in a black suit and Sunday shoes with cravat and hat, he took his family on the town, promenading before all, asserting his identity as "a civilized man with roots." He could have been anywhere, but in fact he was in Butte, Bear Creek, Red Lodge, and Washoe. It did not matter; whether in clothing, in eating habits, in home furniture, reading material, or entertainment, few compromises were made. If fashion demanded New York knickers in gray tweed with dark caps, then tweed knickers and dark caps it was, in Havre and in Dillon and in Two Dot—however out of place, however inappropriate they may have been.

Today we are apt to see something ludicrous in this, something pretentious in hauling pianos, dressing "up," and lengthy Sunday dinners. We should not. The ceremonial was disproportionately important and precisely because the distance between ideal and reality was greater than it is today. That distance needed more optimism and greater hope to be bridged. Ceremony helped. Refusing to compromise, homemakers in Montana looked to a future without cultural dilution and one that was permanent.

Underlying all the frenetic, violent, raw, and dramatic impressions left to posterity by these working pioneers is the powerful current of people making homes and fathering towns. When reduced to its essence, Montana's history is the history of house and home. And it is precisely this urge for the family to prevail with civility, to be "at home" with permanence and constancy, that structured so much of society. Historians have paid too little attention to this common concern for home. Perhaps that is natural; it was not dramatic, and it was often obscured. Nevertheless, it was what mattered most to the people who were there—and therefore it should matter to us. Family, home, civilization, and self-improvement—these were the bench marks against which everything was measured.

Homemakers in front of sod house. Dagmar, Montana. *Courtesy Montana Historical Society.*

Two-story frame house with sash windows and chimney. Syverud homestead, East Coalridge Community. *H. B. Syverud, photographer. Courtesy Montana Historical Society.*

Unusual Victorian family portrait. Fred Miller family, Hardin, Montana, ca. 1908. *F. Miller, photographer. Courtesy Hulda Fields.*

Assembled family at Philipsburg, Montana, ca. 1900. *Courtesy University of Montana Archives.*

"Out for a Sunday drive."
Philipsburg, Montana, ca.
1900. *Courtesy University of Montana Archives.*

"White parasol and black cow." Bear Creek, Montana, ca. 1915. *Courtesy Mrs. Jesse Cameron.*

Dressed up for the circus. Missoula, Montana, 1908. *Courtesy University of Montana Archives.*

Mission Hotel in St. Ignatius, Montana, with opera house in background. *Courtesy Tim Gordon.*

Interior of opera house, Philipsburg, Montana. *Courtesy William E. Farr.*

Theatre production of "Kaiser Bill." Finnish Brotherhood Hall, Red Lodge, Montana, ca. 1917. *Courtesy Mrs. Huovinen.*

Opposite page: Finnish Athletic Club, Red Lodge, Montana, 1915. Courtesy Mrs. Tom Ladvala. This page: Women and style. Lewiston, Montana. Courtesy Ford Knight.

"Ready for a Sunday drive with the family." Dutton, Montana, ca. 1920. *Courtesy George Sollid.*

Boy Scouts selling liberty bonds. Belt, Montana, 1917. *Courtesy Great Falls Public Library.*

W.C.T.U. entry in the Fourth of July parade. "All in white." Columbus, Montana, 1916. *Courtesy James T. Annin.*

A small schoolhouse in western Montana. *Courtesy University of Montana Archives.*

Public school interior, Woodworth, Montana, 1915. *Courtesy University of Montana Archives.*

Left, above: Consolidated school wagons for bussing farm children. Victor, Montana. *Courtesy Henry Grant. Left, below:* "Decoration Day Celebration" in Darby, Montana. *Courtesy Henry Grant. Right:* Beautification — ladies planting trees at Fort Missoula. Missoula, Montana, ca. 1910. *Courtesy University of Montana Archives.*

May Day on the plains. Browning, Montana, ca. 1915. *Courtesy Sherburne Collection.*

"Bringing in a Badlands Cedar for Christmas." Brockway, Montana, ca. 1928. *Courtesy Phillip Haglund.*

Christmas in Havre, ca. 1910. *Courtesy Al Lucke.*

Left: Christmas at the ranch. Circle, Montana, 1913. *Courtesy Verna Carlson.*
Below: "Home for Christmas." Missoula, Montana. *Courtesy University of Montana Archives.*

University of Montana with tennis courts and stadium. Missoula, Montana. *Morton J. Elrod, photographer. Courtesy University of Montana Archives.*

Funeral procession with horses veiled in black. Havre, Montana, 1908. *Courtesy Al Lucke.*

Members of the United Protestant drive for the Deaconess Hospital in Havre, Montana. *Courtesy Al Lucke.*

Red Cross campaign for war effort. Red Lodge, Montana, ca. 1917. *Courtesy James T. Annin.*

Sherburne family at their retreat. Many Glacier, Montana, 1905. *Courtesy Sherburne Collection.*

"Cook car for the big outfits." Buffalo, Montana. *Courtesy "In the Shadow of the Twin Sisters," published by Montana Business Service.*

Family portrait. W. R. Freeman and family, Bear Creek, Montana.
Courtesy Mrs. Jesse Cameron.

Adoring mother. Mrs. W. R. Freeman and Bill, Bear Creek, Montana, ca. 1920. *Courtesy Mrs. Jesse Cameron.*

Sunday at Columbia Gardens. Butte, Montana, 1900. *Courtesy World Museum of Mining, Butte, Montana.*

May Day celebration. *Courtesy University of Montana Library.*

The Homesteaders

After they had left, they were called honyockers, bohunks, nesters, and scissorbills—and if the terms were obscure in origin, they were clearly pejorative and used with derision. But while they were here (in eastern and central Montana), they were called homesteaders, and for the entire region they represented an ebullient hope for progress and prosperity.

Between about 1900 and 1917, roughly eighty thousand of them flooded into eastern and central Montana. By 1924, sixty thousand had moved out; behind them, they left eleven thousand deserted farms, more than one hundred deserted towns, two hundred and fourteen failed banks, millions of eroded acres, farm mortgage indebtedness of $175 thousand, and a drop in the per acre value of farmland of $320 million.

Perhaps it was the nature and awesome consequence of this massive exodus that resulted (until very recently) in the "blanking out" of this period in the histories of Montana and the Dakotas. People have an aversion to the process of examining dark and tragic events of their pasts.

Yet this *was* America's last real frontier; it *was* the last siren call of free land—and for whatever reasons, the honyockers came, and whatever may be said of their ignorance of the raw malevolence of the land to which they came, they were a people of great courage, tenacity, strength, and determination. It is historically unconscionable to ignore their ordeal.

They came in a rush that began in about 1900, due to a series of circumstances which fell into place with a kind of random fortuity. Land prices, particularly in the Middle-West, had skyrocketed; in 1909, the Congress passed the Enlarged Homestead Act that provided *free* land in 320-acre plots on the public domain in the West. In eastern Montana alone, there were 41 million such acres—free for the filing and the taking. No one told the homesteaders that 320 acres on the vast, flat, semi-arid, brown midriff of America was equal (with luck) to about thirty acres of the deep-loamed land of Illinois or Virginia or Pennsylvania or to the rich soil of Minnesota or the eastern Dakotas.

For thousands of years, the Great Plains have been characterized by alternating cycles of "wet" and "dry" periods—which is really to say, periods of precipitation marginal for the dry-land growing of wheat (15 inches per year) alternating approximately every twenty to thirty years with periods of withering drought (4 inches per year). But no one told the homesteader that—and the years between 1900 and 1917 were "wet" ones. Excellent high protein wheat could be grown, and it was.

With the passage of the Enlarged Homestead Act, the western railroads, chambers of commerce, and land speculators or "locators" began a massive national campaign to attract settlers to this "Eden of America." They were often joined by the ranchers in Montana and the Dakotas, because the price of cattle had plummeted, but the price of land was climbing. It was a campaign conducted with great skill and little or no involvement with facts. It was sustained, clever, and well financed—and it represented a working partnership between state governments, railroads, developers, booster organizations of all sorts, chambers of commerce, and con men. And it worked—and they came.

The western railroads had changed *everything* in Montana as of 1883. The Northern Pacific reached eastern Montana first. Hard on its heels came the Utah Northern which probed up from Ogden to Butte; then in 1893, James J. Hill's Great Northern cut swiftly across the northern immensity of the state.

If the railroads changed the cattle, lumbering, mining, and merchandising businesses, they wrought the greatest change in eastern Montana and with respect to the homesteaders' frontier. It started with James J. Hill and the Great Northern. It was Hill's intent to see that eight thousand farms replaced the one hundred and fifty or so ranches which characterized the land through which the railroad passed. He began a gigantic "railroad colonization" plan. He was quickly joined by the Northern Pacific and the Chicago, Milwaukee and St. Paul.

One-way "settler's fares" from St. Paul to Billings were cut to twelve dollars and fifty cents. A man or a family could rent an entire box car for only fifty dollars. The railroads produced hundreds of thousands of glowing brochures which they distributed in the Middle-West and East. They ran "exhibition trains," demonstrating with great golden shocks of wheat how rich and fertile the soils of eastern Montana were. It was marvelously successful.

They came by the thousands in coaches, boxcars, a few Model Ts—to Bainville, Havre, Miles City, Big Timber, Forsythe, Hobson, Big Sandy, and Geraldine. They brought pitifully little with them—except for an abundance of hope, youth, muscle, determination, and courage. They fanned off across the endless sea of land, and they filed on their homesteads or borrowed from the local bank and bought acreage from ranchers.

While the wet cycle lasted, they performed wonders. In 1900, there had been 7 thousand farms in the eastern counties of Montana. By 1920, there were 46 thousand. In 1909, only 250 thousand acres were producing wheat; by 1919, this had risen to 35 million acres! The homesteaders built nearly one hundred new towns—raw, utilitarian, and ugly. They were startlingly alike—one street, the lumberyard, the granary, the bank, the school, the general store, and the church. There were few, if any, bars.

But the homesteaders did not live there. They lived perhaps fifteen or twenty miles away, on "the place." And the "places" were startlingly alike, too. The house, usually 24 feet by 24 feet, was made of green lumber; tar paper was tacked on the outside; newspapers were glued with flour and water paste to the inside wall for insulation. The glowing reports of the promoters had neglected to mention that winter temperatures often reached 25° below zero. There was a cook stove, bunks, a couple of chairs, and sometimes two rooms, usually separated by a curtain. Indoor plumbing was rare. Since the water table was often five hundred feet down, the water supply was sometimes a cistern. The "epizootic" was common. So was typhoid.

Though most generalized accounts of the homestead era deal with the awesomely cold winters and dwell on the shortage of fuel (buffalo chips, twisted grass bundles, or, in extremes, the burning of fence posts and barn siding), photographs tell another story. The entire area of eastern Montana and western North Dakota is underlaid by coal. The veins are usually close to the surface or completely exposed in gullies or arroyos. Most homesteaders had abundant supplies of coal.

While it is true that the homesteader's shack was usually primitive indeed, such was not always the case. There is near Lavine an Iowa farm, literally recreated or transplanted to the semi-arid plains. Notice the silos, the windmill, the corn-belt machinery, the corn binder, the corn cultivator, the ensilage cutter, and the manure spreader. Obviously this farmer tried everything: corn, hogs, steer feeding, wheat—and doubtless, barley and oats. But Lavina was not Sioux City; Montana was not Iowa. So, in these photographs, the empty buildings lie baking in the sun. Maybe, if we could hear it, a dry, hot wind stirs under the eaves of the barn. In the photograph of the tractor and the machine shed, notice the earth; it is seared. Only a few scraggly weeds survive on that entire section (640 acres) purchased in hope from the Northern Pacific Railroad.

But that was after the collapse. Now, in the good time, the homesteader plowed in the spring, planted, prayed for rain; in the fall, he harvested and hauled his wheat to the granary in high, heavy-wheeled wagons drawn by his one team. And then, almost invariably, he went to the bank—not usually to pay, but to borrow. And the bankers obliged—at ten percent. The honyocker needed more land, more seed. The crop had been good—maybe fifty bushels per acre. The price of wheat was good.

The banker was not worried; he usually knew little about banking. All he knew was that the war in Europe was sending the price of wheat to unprecedented levels, that crops were very good, that the town was growing. In more than fifty percent of the honyocker banks, loans exceeded deposits by spectacular margins. For instance, the bank in Fort Benton had deposits of $702,000 and loans of $1,427,000. Most of the loan money was on next year's crop. But the banker was not worried. The answer was clear—more land, more seed. And another answer was clearer still—mechanization.

It was in the early teens that the tractors came, huge steel-wheeled, giant-spoked, steam snorters (or kerosene burners)—and they changed everything. From dawn to dusk, with the water wagon pulled alongside by a team of horses, the giant tractor could plow in a day what a good team could plow in two weeks. It took forty barrels of water per day—and where to find the water? But a big tractor could pull seven fully loaded grain wagons with no effort. Technology had come to the plains. The potential beggared the mind—and the actuality ripped up millions of terribly fragile acres.

Maybe only the old-time rancher dating back to the 1870s knew the folly of it. There is some evidence of that, but it is sparse. It is not sparse in retrospect. This huge and burgeoning empire rested solely on the arrival of the proper moisture at the proper time. The honyocker, the banker, the merchant, all the people in the new towns—all the hopes and dreams and plans rested solely on an upside down pyramid. One might call it a giant gamble, except that there was really no gamble at all—no odds. The plains would do what the plains had done for (we now know) thousands of years. They would host the drought on schedule. For drought on the Great Plains is not an aberrance, as even to this day we consider it to be. It is inherent in the very nature of the plains. Nor is it a simple process; it is infinitely complex.

It began, on this occasion, in north-central Montana in 1917, one hot, glowing spot. Havre registered 0.33 of an inch in May and only 0.45 in June, the wet month. The humid' hovered near 4 percent. In 1918, the heat spread southward and eastward; by 1919, it burned fiercely in all of eastern Montana and western North and South Dakota. With the heat and dryness, there came, as there always had, sustained hot winds, vast range fires—and grasshoppers. The insects came in endless blankets of obscene black clouds, clacking, whirring, and devouring everything from wheat to shingles. On the advice of agronomists, the honyockers chopped up lemons, mixed the rinds with arsenic and cast it all about them. The hoppers ate it and clacked on. The honyockers built hopper fences; they used beaters; they piled dead hoppers into haystack-like piles and burned them. Many of the roads were impassable because they were covered several feet deep in the slippery mass of dead hoppers. Trains could not run because the tracks were too slippery.

In the towns, the blowing, powdered earth permeated every crack and cranny. It reddened the eyes and gritted in the teeth—and across millions of acres, the wheat stubble turned from brown to black and from black to dust and blew eastward on the edge of the hot, gray wind.

The exodus began. They left on the rods of boxcars; they left in Model T's. They left the dying towns, and their houses withered, leaned, and fell down. They went in all directions, on trains, in dilapidated trucks, in wagons, and sometimes on foot. By 1924, about 60 thousand of them had disappeared from Montana.

A few remained; a few are still here. They survived because, quixotically, the drought skipped some areas—or was less severe, or because a nearby spring somehow continued to flow. And they had diversified—a garden, chickens, bone-lean pigs, a milk cow fed on "thistle hay." They ate rattlesnakes and porcupines and made boiled weed soup. And thus they survived until, at last, the "wet" cycle came again.

And what of the land? It never really recovered—except where irrigation projects were instituted. It reverted, for the most part, to the cattlemen. But the range land was not the same. The rich, high-protein native grasses never survived the plow. Erosion took a terrible toll.

Slowly, in some areas, the ranchers have bound up some of the wounds with fertilizer, crop rotation, the introduction of new, tough grasses, and constant attention to all the aspects of conservation. But no one familiar with that land can view it today and fail to see the scars.

There is, of course, a moral. Men cannot ask any land to be what it cannot be and do what it cannot do. It would seem that if we are learning that lesson at all, we are learning it at a perilously slow rate.

Homestead locaters on the Montana Hiline. *Courtesy Donald Carpenter.*

The Sneen and Knutson cronies at Bert Wagnild's shack. Outlook, Montana, July 1911. *Courtesy Mrs. Vernon Stoner.*

Unloading emigrant wagon, including household goods, machinery, four horses, and chickens at Sumatra, Montana, ca. 1913. *H. B. Syverud, photographer. Courtesy Montana Historical Society.*

"Begun with determination." Miles City, Montana. *Courtesy Muriel Cooksey.*

"Ladies at home outside Glasgow, Montana." *Courtesy University of Montana Archives.*

"Ladies at home outside Glasgow, Montana." *Courtesy University of Montana Archives.*

"Dryland Wheat." One of Montana's most important contributions to the war effort, ca. 1917. *Courtesy James T. Annin.*

Early kerosene tractor drawing grain wagons. Havre, Montana, ca. 1910. *Courtesy Al Lucke.*

New homesteaders arriving for the opening of the Flathead Indian Reservation, 1910-1912. St. Ignatius, Montana. *Herman Schnitzmeyer, photographer. Courtesy University of Montana Archives.*

Above: Eastern Montana, ca. 1900. *Courtesy Montana Historical Society. Right:* High prices for wheat during war years. Big Sandy, Montana, 1916. *Courtesy Montana Historical Society.*

Left: The pride of the Danish immigrant family — just-purchased Case tractor. Dagmar, Montana, 1917. *Courtesy Montana Historical Society. Below:* Cutting ice on the Yellowstone River near Miles City. *R. C. Morrison, photographer. Courtesy Mrs. Richard Smith.*

Milwaukee Road engine at the foot of Main Street in Geraldine, Montana, 1915. *Courtesy Public Relations Department, Milwaukee Railroad.*

Above: J. Reo Bird, Bozeman Methodist minister. *Courtesy Museum of the Rockies. Right:* Hutterite children. Glacier County, Montana. *Courtesy Montana State University Archives.*

A squatter in eastern Montana.
Courtesy Montana Historical Society.

Elaborate cook car for the big outfits.
Near Buffalo, Montana. *Courtesy "In
the Shadow of the Twin Sisters,"
published by Montana Business
Service.*

"Dryland farming techniques explained." Eastern Montana. *Both photographs: Courtesy Montana Historical Society.*

Digging a winter's supply of coal. Allen's Vein, Sand Springs, Montana, 1914. *H. B. Syverud, photographer. Courtesy Montana Historical Society.*

Harsh beginnings. *No credit available.*

Mother and child on "the place." Popular, Montana. *Courtesy Donald Carpenter.*

Northern Pacific promotional special extolling dryland wheat farming and the opportunity of agricultural land in eastern Montana, ca. 1910-1920. *Both photographs: Courtesy University of Montana Archives.*

The grasshopper campaign of 1917. A mixing bee for the cutting and grinding of lemons to be mixed with mash and arsenic, then spread on fields to combat grasshoppers or mormon crickets. *Courtesy Montana State University Archives.*

In addition to drought, the plague: mormon crickets. *Courtesy Montana State University Archives.*

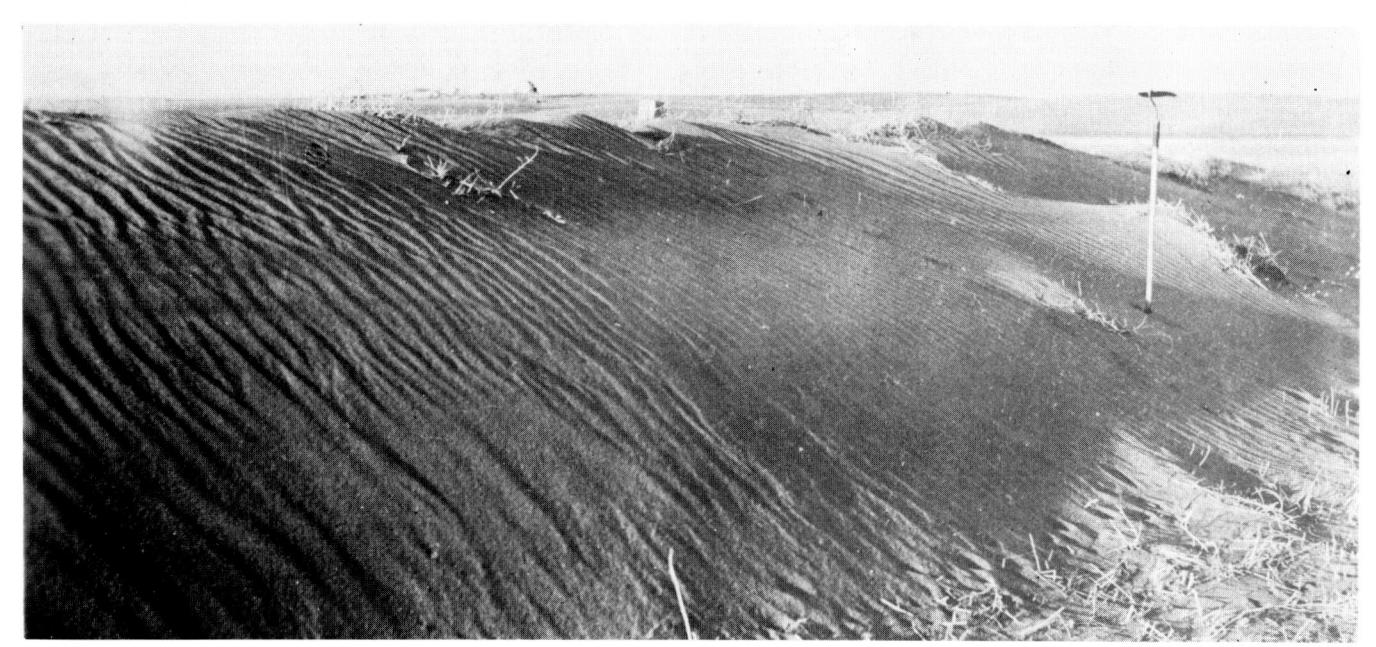

Left, above: Drought plus blowing soil. *H. B. Syverud, photographer. Courtesy Montana Historical Society. Left, below:* The banks failed and people moved on. Charlo, Montana, 1920. *Courtesy University of Montana Archives. Above:* "Leaving." The exodus out of Montana begins. *Courtesy University of Montana Archives.*

Left, Geneva Fornell at LeRoy Spring, Circle, Montana. *Courtesy Verna Carlson. Below,* Ernest and Niels Anderson, Circle, Montana, 1915. *Courtesy Verna Carlson.*

People Having Fun

Wherever Montanans put themselves down upon the enormous land, they quickly and ingeniously developed ways to entertain and amuse themselves. People worked hard, but they also saw to it that they had fun. That ingenuity is beautifully illustrated over and over again in the paintings of Charles M. Russell.

In the chill of an early fall morning, in the days of the open range, the horses were, to put it mildly, lively. The famous painting "Bronc to Breakfast," shows a cowboy half on, half off his bucking horse, scattering the breakfast fire. His companions, seated in the background, are grinning widely. They had been waiting for this—waiting, in fact, to cheer the horse and jeer the man. It was as traditional as it was fun.

Other Russell paintings show cowboys roping grizzly bears—one roper going for the head, the other for the hind feet. This required, in fact, not only roping skill but great agility by horse and rider. An enraged grizzly was nothing to fool around with. And while bears were a little uncommon, cowboys always seemed to find something to rope—if nothing else, a running coyote.

People had fun at what they knew best, their work. For the cowboy, the principal vehicle for fun was, naturally enough, the horse. Games revolved around racing or strength. The short-coupled cow horses raced short dashes down the main street of town or around several blocks. The races drew huge crowds and the betting was often heavy. There were also roping contests and other horse-centered games—all of which in due course led to the elaborate rodeo. One of those games was the "horse-pulling" contest—a lariat was strung between two horses and riders, snubbed tightly around the saddle horn as each tried to pull the opponent across a line in a tug of war. A great deal of pride rested on the outcome.

Farmers had a different kind of "horse-pulling" event. They took their huge work horses, the "Shires" as they were often called generically, and had them pull dead weight on sleds from a standing start for a given distance in a given time. Here there was heavy money bet on heavy horses. Nothing demonstrated raw muscular power quite like these contests, yet there was also something strangely beautiful about a matched team of Clydesdales rhythmically pulling tons of dead weight.

Other occupations contributed their own special diversions. Hard-rock miners in Butte and the mining towns competed fiercely with one another in public single and double "hand-drilling" contests. "Mucking" races, based on the miner's task of loading ore cars, proliferated and grew to world-champion proportions and status. City firemen, so proud of their skill and their speed in laying hose or scaling buildings, raced each other and the firemen of neighboring towns. Everywhere working men and women honed their occupational skills to a competitive edge in order to entertain themselves and their communities. But they could also laugh at themselves and their specialized dress and specialized skills. What, for example, could be more humorous than a bandy-legged cowboy in high-heels, spurs, chaps, and devoid of horse, down on the ground running a footrace. It was high occupational humor.

Beyond the competitive games, there was just plain entertainment often associated with the exotic. The circus came to town, and it came on its own brightly painted train. A place on the edge of town was chosen, and the great elephants moved ponderously down the plank ramps from the cars. They did most of the work—and most excited the kids. The luckiest youngsters got free tickets for watering the pachyderms or the camels or the lions—and for them, that was more thrilling than the circus itself. Once set up, there was the inevitable circus parade through town. Nobody who could walk or hobble missed it.

And almost every summer, the Gypsies came. This was a mixed matter. Gypsies, after all, were truly exotic. Besides, they were thought to be born thieves, and a goodly number of obstreperous town children had been repeatedly warned that Gypsies stole children who did not behave. While some sheriffs ran the Gypsies off, most did not. They simply watched them closely. After all, the gaily painted wagons, often with dancing bears chained to them, were intriguingly unusual. So were the costumes, the frenetic dances, and, above all, the dark-eyed fortune tellers. Most people who visited the Gypsy camp carefully pinned their wallet pockets shut, and women clutched their purses to their breasts. It was thrilling. Everyone knew that Gypsies were the most celebrated pickpockets in the world.

Minstrel shows were another exotic attraction. There were two kinds: white minstrels in black-face, and black minstrels, often in white-face. There was an invariable format: banjo, tambourines, trumpet, and trombone; the "strut" dance, the "straight" men, and the comics. But, somehow, like vaudeville, it never grew old.

There were other ways to entertain and amuse. In the early western towns of Montana, and in the eastern cattle towns (as distinct from homesteader towns), saloons were much in evidence, and heavy drinking, especially during the long winter months, was at most a venial transgression. Gambling was wide open. However, three-card monte, strap game, thimberling game, patent safe game, black and red, any dice game, and two card faro were all regarded as "legally unfair."

The homesteading communities of the east were different. There were fewer bars there and much less drinking. But there was an overwhelming variety of get-togethers to swim, to picnic, to learn the latest farming techniques from the extension agent, to put up hay, to raise a barn, or to build a church. There were 4th of July tug-of-war contests, sack races, three-legged races, band concerts, and county fairs. Above all were the county fairs, where both information and gossip floated about; where ladies competed with each other in baking, canning, and quilting; and where elaborate booths offered agricultural pride a place to exhibit. Excitement existed there; it was ambient, it teased every sense, breaking the long monotony of summer labor.

In a land in which hunting was once at the very core of survival, it may seem odd to add hunting and fishing to the category of recreation. But, again, the old photographs insist that men and women spent long, pleasant hours outdoors, fishing cold lakes and rushing streams, or tramping after game. Others put up with hardship even in their leisure, a trait which we find hard to comprehend—they, of course, were outdoor people, while most of us are not. Hunting and fishing, always popular, grew to amazing proportions as a form of recreation, and that has not changed with the years, at least not in Montana.

There was another form of "recreation" which may seem a little strange to us today. It was "politics." In the 1880s and 1890s when William Andrews Clark and Marcus Daly were in a bitter contest with each other for control of the state's political machinery, campaigns were not merely characterized by bribery and fraud—they were bacchanalian celebrations in which millions of dollars were spent to "entertain the voters." The mines and the woods camps closed (which meant that practically the whole of the state was shut down) while hundreds of barrels of whiskey were sent out to the woods camps. In the towns, the drinks were "on the house," that is, paid for by Clark or Daly. The entertainment was expensive and the results bizarre. Literally a whole state went on periodic binges and later suffered massive hangovers. Political history was made in at least one respect. In several elections, many precincts reported a voter turnout of 120 to 130 percent.

When national politicians, William Jennings Bryan or Theodore Roosevelt, for instance, campaigned in Montana, they encountered massive crowds. But they also had their problems. Their voices could rarely be heard over the cacophany of the raucous people who came for the fun of it—to see and be seen.

There was a "higher" form of entertainment, too. The mining magnates built "spas" as plush and elaborate as any in Europe. Two prime examples were the magnificently opulent Broadwater Hotel, just west of Helena, and the Turkish-like spa at Gregson Hot Springs. Such establishments featured oriental rugs, magnificent mahogany paneling, parqueted floors constructed of every exotic wood imaginable, huge indoor swimming pools, and splendidly ornate fountains and cascades. The "common people" could not afford the spas.

They *could* afford the boxing matches. And the fights took place everywhere—indoors, outdoors, summer and winter. Boxing in Montana reached its apogee in 1923 at Shelby when Jack Dempsey defeated Tommy Gibbons on a hot 4th of July. That a fight of this importance could take place in the small town of Shelby may have been a tribute to the long-held interest of Montanans in boxing, but more plausibly, its explanation lies in the ingenuity of its promoters and the wild enthusiasm of the citizens of the town. That it was utterly disastrous financially does not detract from the fact that whatever Shelby was, is, or will be—the Dempsey-Gibbons fight assures its place in history.

When the automobile came, it changed recreation as it changed everything else. There were, of course, races. But the real fun lay in tours—ten or twelve machines to the tour. Due to the very unpredictability of the machines and the roads, it was high adventure.

And then came the airplane. It had very little practical application, but it was *fun*. The term "barnstorming" is precisely descriptive. These intrepid flyers came out among us, landed in pastures, kept the machine in the barn overnight, put an ad in the local paper and took the bravest of the brave tilting and tipping up into the sky for five dollars apiece. It was nearly as much fun to watch as to ride.

The barnstormers became regulars at fairs. They started their show with hair-raising acrobatics and finished with five-dollar rides over the town. Their business was always brisk.

One day in 1929, the *Billings Gazette* announced that the world's largest airplane would land at the airport—a Ford Trimotor. Let an eye witness describe it:

> It came in from the north and it was so huge you could see it twenty miles away. When its enormous bulk glided smoothly to the ground one

could see that it was made of corrugated metal. *Metal!* How could that enormous weight remain airborne? And yet, its three huge engines churning and rattling the ear drums, it took off as smoothly as a gull.

Yes, and the airplane was really fun no more. It was no longer varnished silk glued on wood. The wind no longer whistled in the wires of its wings; its engine no longer sputtered, died, and then coughed to life again—maybe. The airplane was a business now and the fun was gone.

No matter. Wherever a people settle, upon whatever kind of land, however harsh, they will find something to have fun with—and if there is really nothing there at all, they will have fun simply by getting together.

Horse-pulling contest in the center of town. Blackfeet Indian Reservation. Browning, Montana, July 1907. *Courtesy Sherburne Collection.*

Horse-pulling contest, Blackfeet Indian Reservation, Browning, Montana, July 1907. *Courtesy Sherburne Collection.*

Cowboy foot race at the 101 Ranch Rodeo. Sidney, 1919. *Courtesy J. K. Ralston Museum.*

Left: Cowboys on the town drinking "Grain Belt" beer. Eastern Montana, ca. 1900. *Courtesy Montana State University Archives. Below:* Cowboys drinking beer and eating homemade ice cream. *Courtesy Montana State University Archives.*

In front of the saloon. *Courtesy Montana State University Archives.*

"The party's over." Bitterroot Valley, ca. 1912. *Courtesy Henry Grant.*

Texas cowhands playing cards on roundup near Fallon, Montana, 1908. *John L. Breum, photographer. Courtesy J. H. Trafton.*

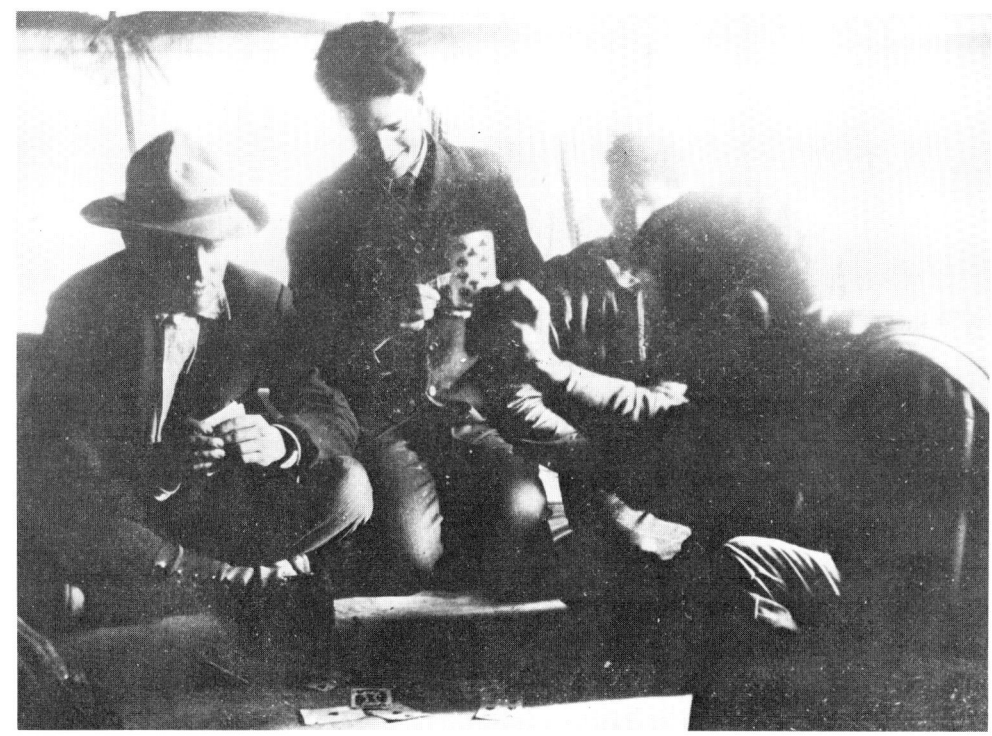

Recreation at the United States Reclamation Service camp on Terror Creek. Babb Diversion Project, Babb, Montana, 1905. *Courtesy Sherburne Collection.*

Left: double hand-drilling champions. Butte, Montana. *Courtesy Al Hooper. Above:* Butte firemen demonstrating their skill with hose and nozzle. Butte, Montana. *Courtesy Tim Gordon.*

Balloon ascension at Glendive, Montana. *A. S. Foss, photographer. Courtesy M. L. Graves.*

Circus parade in downtown Missoula. Missoula, Montana, ca. 1905. *Courtesy William E. Farr.*

Left: Norris and Rowe's Shows. Missoula, Montana, ca. 1905. *Courtesy William E. Farr. Above:* "Gollman Bros. Circus about 1916 going down Second Ave." Wolfpoint, Montana. *Courtesy Donald Carpenter.*

Left: Minstrel show in tent. Miles City, Montana. R. C. Morrison, photographer. Courtesy Mrs. Richard Smith. *Above:* Gypsy camp with bear outside of Glasgow, Montana. Courtesy University of Montana Archives.

Teddy Roosevelt speaking in Butte. *Courtesy Museum of the Rockies.*

William Jennings Bryan in Hamilton with Marcus Daly on platform. 1896. *Courtesy Henry Grant.*

"A good catch." Fishing on Lake Sherburne near Babb, Montana. 1910. *Courtesy Sherburne Collection.*

Fishermen and dog. Havre, Montana, ca. 1900. *Courtesy Al Lucke.*

Coyotes, mountain lions, and sheep. Sula, Montana. *Courtesy Henry Grant.*

Packing out mountain sheep, ca. 1910. *Courtesy University of Montana Archives.*

Ladies having lunch at Camp Retreat. Lake Sherburne. *Courtesy Sherburne Collection.*

Sunday afternoon target practice. Dutton, Montana, 1915. *Courtesy George Sollid.*

Interior of saloon and licensed gambling place. Stanford, Montana Territory, ca. 1880s. *Courtesy Al Lucke.*

Funeral at the Broadwater in Helena, Montana. *Courtesy Ford Knight.*

Turkish elegance at Gregson Hot Springs. *Courtesy University of Montana Archives.*

Right: Intercollegiate track meet. University of Montana, Missoula, Montana, ca. 1910. *Morton J. Elrod, photographer. Courtesy University of Montana Archives. Below:* "James Bad Marriage turning the corner." Blackfeet Indian Reservation. Browning, Montana, ca. 1910. *Courtesy Montana Historical Society.*

Above: Playing ball at the cistern pump. Near Circle, Montana, ca. 1918. *Courtesy Verna Carlson.* *Left:* The Dutton girls' team. Dutton, Montana, 1909. *Courtesy George Sollid.*

Right: "Lumber camp boxing." Bonner, Montana, ca. 1910. *Courtesy University of Montana Archives.* *Above:* World Championship Boxing — Jack Dempsey-Tommy Gibbons fight in Shelby, Montana, July 4, 1923. *Courtesy Great Falls Public Library.*

Page 244, upper photograph: Three-legged race at Homesteader picnic. Eastern Montana, ca. 1915. *Courtesy Montana State Archives. Page 244, lower photograph:* "Swimming in Sage Creek near Packer's Ranch." 1930. *Courtesy University of Montana Archives. Page 245, upper photograph:* Loggers swimming after work. Western Montana, ca. 1920. *Courtesy University of Montana Archives. Page 245, lower photograph:* "Tug of War at picnic on Carlson Ranch." Circle, Montana. *Courtesy Verna Carlson. Above:* "Spectators at the circus." *Courtesy University of Montana Archives.*

"Picnic at Medicine Lake. Fresh fried fish was enjoyed." 1926. *Courtesy Montana Historical Society.*

"Fun on the Chute." Savage, Montana, 1912. *Courtesy J. K. Ralston Museum.*

Kids returning on street car from Columbia Gardens. Butte, Montana. *Courtesy Al Hooper.*

Barney Oldfield racing airplane at Missoula Fairgrounds. Missoula, Montana, 1915. *Courtesy John E. Fox.*

How's the Road?

If one were to search the best reference works in the best libraries under the heading "transportation," one could compile a bibliography of mind-boggling length. There are literally thousands of studies of railroads, river steamboats, canal barges, stagecoaches, and freight wagons.

Yet the advent of the automobile has been largely ignored by historians. If the railroad or steamboats or other methods of getting from here to there changed demographic patterns and had significant economic and social effects, the coming of the automobile brought about a revolution—economic, social, cultural, and demographic. It was a revolutionary event not only in that it profoundly altered almost all of our ways of doing things, but because it also came very quickly. In 1900, motive power was the horse; by 1915, it was the internal combustion engine.

At root, the revolution was simple: there suddenly occurred an awesome shrinking of space—and concomitantly, a shrinkage of time. Remote places were suddenly no longer remote. Distances had been measured by the speed of a horse—about six miles per hour—for centuries. The location of cities, towns, way stations, schools; the movement of armies, the movement of food, merchandise, of every conceivable thing—all were determined by how far a horse could travel in a day. Suddenly that measurement was anachronistic, and nothing would ever be the same again.

Which came first, the really functional automobile or the road? The answer is—the automobile. This led to some bizarre transitions and a whole series of new governmental structures. As has always been the case, one basic technological breakthrough led swiftly and inexorably to an almost explosive series of new pressures, new industries, and new problems.

In the beginning, the begoggled and aproned automobile driver, hanging on for dear life to a sturdy steering wheel, used the "roads" that were there. But they were hardly suitable for a machine which could reach the blinding speed of thirty miles per hour. Those were horse roads, wagon roads. The problems seemed simply insurmountable. First there was the mud, the gumbo. The automobile owner quickly discovered that he could not drive after a rain or through naturally boggy areas.

He did not invent the "corduroy" system, but he quickly adapted it to his needs. He laid logs across the mud. If they sank, he laid more logs until, at last, he could charge violently over the gumbo area and go reeling on his way.

In some areas, planks were used; usually these measured four feet by twelve feet, and they were heavy and unwieldy. After counties had more or less taken over the responsibility for roads, county crews would sometimes stack the planks beside the road in dry weather, or place them in bogs in wet weather. More often than not, however, this back-breaking job was up to the driver himself.

But, then there were the rocks. The problem lay in the tires. They were either solid rubber—in which event his machine was literally shaken to pieces and the road behind him was littered with bolts, nuts, and sundry parts, or they were "fabric" tires. In the latter case (because there was no "ply" in these early tires), the driver was forever having "flats." One early automobile dealer in Missoula, H. O. Bell, the proprietor of Montana's first "agency" (1915) remarked, "Well, along about in those years you figured twelve hours to Hamilton (forty-five miles) and back. And you figured seven to eight flats per trip for the full ninety miles. That, of course, was on a good day."

Some "fabric" tires were guaranteed for three thousand miles, but few lasted for more than fifteen hundred. The task of "patching" a tire was heavy work. The tire was pried from the wheel with a sprung leaf. The tube was extracted and the puncture located. The area was roughed with sandpaper, washed with benzine, then coated with rubber cement. The patch was then applied. This was called "cold patching."

"Hot patching" was more complex and was more often done at the local "garage" after the car owner had stored up a half-dozen tubes or so. This was often called "vulcanizing" and involved sealing the patch to the puncture with a clamp and the burning of gun powder to fuse rubber to rubber. The results were somewhat unreliable.

To fix a flat, the driver had to patch tire and tube on the spot. For this operation, he had a remarkable array of tools, usually carried in a commodious tool box on the fender or running board.

Since these early tires carried about seventy pounds of pressure, blowouts (which were frequent) often wrenched the wheel from the driver's hands. Even if rack-and-pinion easy steering had existed then, no driver in his right mind would steer with one hand. He had to be prepared at all times to engage in a fierce battle with the steering wheel.

The so-called "cord" tire came along in 1916. They were a vast improvement, and one might reasonably expect four thousand or even five thousand miles from them. These automobiles carried spares, of course, but they were used only for replacing a broken wheel.

As the machines began to proliferate, the pressure, first on county commissioners and then on the state legislature, became intense. Get into the road-building business—or else. The counties, and then the state, did. There is, sometimes, an awesome power in zealotry. The owners of the very early machines were not merely zealots, they were messianic. Both county and state governments sought to resist them, but their numbers increased startlingly—as did their power.

When Henry Ford's Model T put the automobile within reach of almost everyone ($550), there was no resisting the "good roads" movement. By 1915, the federal government, as was inevitable, got into the act and established the Bureau of Public Roads.

Still, roads were often more like obstacle courses than highways. The automobile, all through the 1920s, was designed to overcome the obstacles. There were few "niceties." A "trip" took some thoughtful preparation: goggles, dusters, tools, food, drinking water—and plenty of water for the "boil-overs."

There were precautions: never wrap your thumb around the crank. The engine was too apt to kick back and break the thumb. And it was sure to kick back if the driver had not retarded the spark lever on the steering wheel. That was part of the checklist.

On many machines (though not the Model T), gasoline was sucked up into the carburetor by a hand pump on the dashboard. There was a pressure gauge.

The driver pumped up the pressure, retarded the spark lever, and jumped quickly out to crank the engine before he lost pressure.

There was no such thing as a synchronized transmission, and so shifting from gear to gear involved "double clutching," skill, timing, strength, and luck. It was for this reason that women seldom drove. They were not considered strong enough for the shifting process.

Hills, accordingly, often had to be studied. Could the driver get a run at it? How many gears might he have to shift down? Should he play it safe and simply get into low gear before he started up?

The Model T had a wondrous shifting system, though somewhat quixotic. The driver shifted with foot pedals. The Model T owner, however, had to study hills a bit differently. By far, the most powerful gear on the Model T was reverse. If, therefore, the hill was formidable the wise driver launched his attack upon it backward.

Some hills were famous as challenges. There was Evaro Hill, northwest of Missoula. One *could* get a run at it, but for most machines, it was a "three-shift" hill. Waterwagon Hill (about thirty miles up the Blackfoot) rose steeply after a sharp left-hand turn, and one could *not* get a run at it. Some of the early machines simply could not make it, in which event, a nearby rancher stood ready with his team and for a five-dollar fee hauled the chagrined travelers to the top. McDonald Pass, just west of Helena, was a "planner's" dream and a neophyte's nightmare. It had everything—long slopes, steep rises, sharp curves, and precipitous drop-offs. For anyone who had made the trip to or from Helena and Missoula, there was a standard question: "And how did you do on the pass?"

Then there were "grades" which may or may not have involved steep hills. But they were very narrow, with precipitous drop-offs. Every mile or so, there was a "passing cut," a wide place scooped out of the hill. The "rules of the road" held that the driver nearest the "passing cut" should back his machine up, but since backing was a tricky business, some very hot arguments often ensued.

Other famous "grades" included Sperry's grade west of Ovando, the Salmon Lake grade (about seven miles long) that followed the east edge of Salmon Lake in the Blackfoot, and the Skalkaho, running up over the Sapphire Range east of Hamilton. Navigating the latter was "an experience" even as late as the early 1940s.

Rain was always a problem, beyond the basic troubles with traction. Many cars had heavy fabric tops. In good weather, these were folded back and two strong men were required for putting the top down or up. There were side curtains of fabric with celluloid windows (commonly called "isinglass"). The trouble with isinglass was that it scratched easily and had a tendency to turn yellow, blue, and red. It also cracked in cold weather.

Then there was the problem of keeping the windshield clear. Wipers, operated by hand, were inadequate, and consequently there were frequent stops to clean the windshield. All kinds of preparations were used to produce a coating which would cause a faster runoff. The most effective was a plug of chewing tobacco. When rubbed across the glass, it produced a satisfactory coating. Lest we think that today our technology has produced the ideal windshield grime remover, not so. The best remover happens to be Coca-Cola.

Initially, "tourism" was an in-state business—and it rapidly became a big business. First, it spawned "gas stations," many of which quickly became mini-garages, each with a resident mechanic. Then it gave rise to motor park camps for those involved in overnight travel. At first, these were tent camps. But these structures quickly gave way to log cabins or to flimsily built board "row cabins." The travelers built their own fires in the stoves and usually carried their own food with them in commodious wicker baskets and elaborate thermos bottles. Showers and bathtubs were rare, and running water was not always available. The word "motel" entered our lexicon at an amazingly late date—the mid-1930s. Yet, of course, these primitive camps were the precursors of the motel business which is today huge and fundamental to our economy.

Just as the "good-roads movement" was a potent force as early as 1915, so was the belief that "tourism" was destined to be one of Montana's basic industries. The messianic supporters of the good-roads movement put constant and dedicated pressure on government—city, county, state, and federal.

They insisted that state (or county) highway departments be created with the power of "eminent domain" (the power of public entity to condemn private property for public use). They were sick, they said, of roads which had to follow section lines or old wagon trails. They demanded bridges, and they were enraged when they had to risk their precious machines to flimsy ferries—and be charged a fee by the ferryman at that. Worse, when the river froze, the ferries stopped. Then the automobile people had to trust the ice. As H. O. Bell remarked, "It wasn't just that you had to trust your machine to the ice; by God, you had to trust lives!"

There was no turning these hot-eyed people away. Automobiling had first become a religion and then a potent economic lobby. Bridges were built, government agencies were established, taxes were levied—and then came another demand—gravel. These roads should be "built up" on a solid boulder or "fill" base. Then they should be covered with crushed rock gravel. Some legislators blanched. They pointed out, logically enough, that there was not even the technology to make gravel. Think of the expense of great "crushers." Think of the *cost*!

Let H. O. Bell, the father of the good-roads movement in Montana, speak again: "Those fellows were blind. We had had stamp mills or crushing mills in Montana in the 1860s. For the Lord's sake, this is a mining state. We had to tell those fellows to take off their blinders. We said, 'Look, the cost is nothing if you figure the profit. It's a whole new industry and a whole new way of doing things. Hell, we'll invent the technology. You fellows just pass the laws—or else.'" And they did.

One of the spin-offs of the good-roads movement was the Park to Park Highway (do not read interstate). The rapidly growing network of roads should be fully connected so that the machines could travel from Glacier to Yellowstone—or vice versa. And it was with this concept that "tourism" in its real sense took root. For the Park to Park Highway was not just for Montanans; it was for all Americans. Montana had two of the greatest national parks in the world. Connect them with a serviceable road and think of what it would mean! Think of the money benefit to the state!

The park people themselves pitched into the cause. They were already running their own bus systems. They had long, sturdy, White buses—open air, chain driven. In the parks themselves there had been frantic road-building programs—with federal money. The big, powerful buses could easily carry fifteen persons. They were "open air" but they had a "canopy" which could be let down in bad weather. They were big—five doors to a side and they were "reliable." The Park to Park Highway was built—or rather, connected. Part of its significance was that the movement signaled the active participation of the federal government, which became *fait accompli* in 1915 with the establishment of the Bureau of Public Roads.

Still, as we flash along the interstate today, the car itself doing most of the driving, air conditioned, a radio giving us the news or a tape deck blasting out Bob

Dylan, with power steering, power brakes, automatic transmission, soft leather cushioning, and comfort of uncommon definition, we forget how short a time ago the automobile, now central to our economy and life style, was a real adventure and a very real challenge.

Consider just this one automobile trip, undertaken in April of 1920, from the Bitterroot Valley to Milestown (Miles City). Let the adventurers report it for themselves via a story in the Miles City *Daily Star* of April 25, 1920. The headline read "HARD TRIP TO MILESTOWN FROM THE BITTERROOT."

W. P. Stephensen, special surveyor, and an assistant, G. L. Siedel, who arrived a couple of days ago from Missoula, to survey unsurveyed homestead land in the Custer forest, had a tough trip, they report, spent more than two weeks on the way, had to dig their Ford truck out of deep snow drifts on the continental divide, were pulled out of numerous mud holes by teams, and as a fitting finale, while climbing the hill on the Moon creek trail, got stuck in the mud Thursday and were forced to make an all night camp.

Mr. Siedel took a few snapshots of the car as it was stuck in mud in the Bitterroot valley east of Missoula. Mud completely hides the wheels from view in the photos, and both of the travelers state that for thirteen miles they were towed by horses until they finally got over the bad road.

Reaching the pass over the summit of the Rockies, they were warned to hold up for a time until the deep snows melted, but wishing to come on through, they kept traveling. The snow had begun to melt, and before going any considerable distance they were overtaken by their Nemesis—the Ford reached an exceptionally soft spot where the snow was about a dozen feet in depth, and dropped almost out of sight, they say.

Help was secured, but it took some labor and several hours' time to get under way again, but it was finally accomplished, and the journey continued. Rain fell during the entire trip, they report, and when they at last reached the Moon creek road and started up the hill, the wheels gummed up with stiff mud, which refused to come off. Camp was made and the mud guards had to be taken off and the wheels scraped before they could make it on into Milestown.

Another member of the surveying party, W. M. Snow, left Missoula shortly after the departure of the truck and traveled here by train. The party plans to leave here as soon as the roads dry up sufficiently to make travel possible, and will journey to the south country to man homestead boundaries. They expect to be gone about 3 months.

It is true that all of our dimensions have been shrunken by this machine and by the great highways which its existence inevitably called forth. But the greatest shrinkage of dimension has not been in miles or time; it has been in our minds. And even beyond that, it has taken place somewhere indefinable within us—somewhere at a visceral core.

The automobile with its speed shattered the stable age-old measurement of distance and time—the horse; we had entered a fourth dimension. The startling thing is that now we have been in that dimension for only a single generation.

Once done, once made, automobiles got better and better and faster and smoother. Or could it be that they—and all of their speedier progeny—got worse and worse, and caused us to lose our place in time and distance? The wonder of it is that we do not know.

Left: "How's the road?" 1912 Empire automobile with two weary, but well equipped, travelers. *Courtesy Museum of the Rockies.* *Below:* "Where's the road?" Trip from Bitterroot Valley to Miles City, Montana, April 1920, with three major hazards: mud, water, and snow. All, however, can be overcome with a little extra horsepower. *Courtesy United States Forest Service, Region One Archives.* *Opposite, both photographs: Courtesy United States Forest Service, Region One Archives.*

Main Street of Kalispell looking south. Automobiles and horses sharing the streets, 1909. *Courtesy Clyde P. Fickes.*

"Bundled up and out for a drive." *Courtesy Museum of the Rockies.*

Changing tire without removing wheel. Near Sidney, Montana, in the summer of 1926 with an old Model T Ford. *Courtesy J. K. Ralston Museum.*

Bailing wire mechanic at work. Eastern Montana, 1920. *Courtesy Mrs. Ruth E. Cameron.*

The Overland in front of ranch house. Circle, Montana. *Courtesy Verna Carlson.*

Everyman a mechanic. Fixing springs, Browning, Montana. *Courtesy Sherburne Collection.*

Temporary halt for indispensable water. Martindale, Montana, ca. 1917. *Courtesy Glacier National Park Archives.*

Tourism at Glacier National Park. Sherburne Lake in Many Glacier area, ca. 1917. *Courtesy Glacier National Park Archives.*

Left: Tour busses at St. Mary's Chalets. Glacier National Park, ca. 1925. *Courtesy Glacier National Park Archives.* Below: "Roosevelt Highway Boosters." Good roads promotion group from Duluth, Minnesota, at Glacier National Park. *Courtesy Montana Historical Society.*

"Park to Park in a Buick." Highway linking Glacier National Park to Yellowstone National Park, 1917. *Courtesy Henry Grant.*

Early Veerac truck of Buttrey's. Havre, Montana, 1910. *Courtesy Al Lucke.*

Oriental Taxi Service. Havre, 1917. *Courtesy Al Lucke.*

Typical garage. John Pipal and a 1926 "Chev" in Pipal's Garage. Wolf Point, Montana. *Courtesy Marvin Presser.*

A new industry — trucking — comes to Montana. Havre, Montana, ca. 1919. *Courtesy Al Lucke.*

Technological breakthrough: balloon tires. Havre, Montana. *Courtesy Al Lucke.*

Dryland farmers from Greenfield Bench near Sun River promoting their interest with an automobile parade. *Courtesy Montana Historical Society.*

More than transportation, more than a toy, and always useful for promotion. *Courtesy Great Falls Public Library.*

A man and his car. A car and its man? J. M. Freeman at Bear Creek, Montana, ca. 1918. *Courtesy Mrs. Jesse Cameron.*

Above: Early pick-up — homemade. Outside Cut Bank, Montana. *Courtesy Al Lucke. Right:* Needing repairs. The ubiquitous Ford. Eureka, Montana, ca. 1919. *Courtesy Lincoln County Library.*

Auto-camping, Philipsburg, Montana. *Courtesy William E. Farr.*

Above: No bridges yet, using the wagon ferry over Yellowstone River. Near Sidney, Montana, 1922. *Courtesy J. K. Ralston Museum. Left:* A great many automobiles and a few people watching rodeo on 101 Ranch, July 4, 1918. The transition in personal transportation from horses to automobiles is complete, and it comes earlier to cow-country than elsewhere. *Courtesy J. K. Ralston Museum.*

Boiling over in Missoula, Montana. *Courtesy Sherburne Collection.*

Above: Picnicking with car. East Glacier. *Courtesy Sherburne Collection.*
Right: Fixing 12 cylinders. East Glacier. *Courtesy Sherburne Collection.*

Above: Cowboy pulling car out of water. East Glacier, Montana. *Courtesy Gary Schmautz.*
Left: "Dusters and Glacier National Park." *Courtesy Sherburne Collection.*

Petroleum: Montana produces and uses. Kremlin well, Kremlin, Montana, 1927. *Courtesy Al Lucke.*

Index

Acculturation, 129, 130, 131
Airplanes, 221, 222
Alder Gulch, 9, 10
"Alice" mine, the, 33
American Fork, 9
Anaconda and Pacific Railroad, 35
Anaconda Copper Mining Company, 35, 61, 62
Anaconda Gold and Silver Mining Company, 34
"Anaconda" mine, the, 34
Automobiles, 96, 221, 251, 252, 253, 254, 255
Automobile tires, 252

Bainville, MT, 196
Bannack, MT, 9
Barnstorming, 221
Bear Creek, MT, 167
Bell, H. O., 252, 254
Benetsee Creek, 9
Big Sandy, MT, 196
Big Timber, MT, 196
Billings, MT, 196
Billings *Gazette*, 221
Bitterroot Valley, 255
Boxing matches, 221
British Columbia, 9
Broadwater Hotel, 221
Brockway, MT, 167
Bryan, William Jennings, 221
Buffalo, 94

Bunyan, Paul, 59
Bureau of Indian Affairs, 131
Bureau of Public Roads, 252, 254
Butte, MT, 11, 13, 33, 34, 35, 166, 167, 196, 219

California, 9, 10, 33, 94
Cameras, 2, 3, 5
Canal barges, 251
Carlson, Verna, 8
Cattle, 196
Cattle drives, roundups, 94, 95
Central City, MT, 9
Chicago, Milwaukee and St. Paul Railroad, 196
Circle, MT, 8
Circle City, MT, 9
Circus, 220
Clark, William Andrews, 221
Coal, 35, 197
Colorado, 9, 94
Cooper, Julia Dean Hayne, 167
Copper, 13, 34, 35, 62
Cowboys, 59, 93, 94, 95, 96, 97, 219, 220; and the open range, 93, 94, 95, 96
Curtis, E. S. 130

Daly, Marcus, 33, 34, 35, 221
Davis, A. J., 34
Dempsey, Jack, 221
Dillon, MT, 167

Dimsdale, Thomas, 11, 12
Drought, 195, 197
Dylan, Bob, 254-55

Eastman, George, 3, 5, 6
Enlarged Homestead Act, 195
Ennis, MT, 167
Eureka, MT, 61
Evaro Hill, 253

Farmers, 59, 96
Finnish Brotherhood Hall, 167
Ford, Henry, 252
Forest fires, 1910, 62-63
Forsythe, MT, 196
Fort Belknap, MT, 131
Fort Benton, MT, 11, 197
Fort Keogh, MT, 131
Freight wagons, 34, 251
Frontier government, 11, 12

Gambling, 219, 220
Games, "having fun," 219, 220, 221, 222
Geraldine, MT, 196
Gibbons, Tommy, 221
Gold Creek, 9
Gold rush, 9, 10, 11, 12, 13, 35, 62, 94
Grasshopper Creek, 9
Grasshoppers, 197, 198
Great Falls, MT, 167
Great Falls *Leader*, 167

277

Great Northern Railroad, 196
Greenbench, MT, 167
Gregson Hot Springs, 221
Gypsies, 220

Haggin, James Ben Ali, 34, 35
Hamilton, MT, 253
Hard winter of 1886-1887, 96
Hardin, MT, 2
Hauser, S. T., 34
Havre, Mt, 7, 167, 196, 197
Hearst, George, 34, 35
Helena *Radiator*, 167
Helena, MT, 10, 11, 62, 167, 221, 253
Hill, James J., 196
Hobson, MT, 196
Holter, A. M. 62
Homemakers, 165, 166, 167, 168
Homesteaders (honyockers), 7, 59, 94, 195, 196, 197, 198, 220
Huffman, L. A., 2, 5

Idaho, 9
Illinois, 195
Indians, 7, 129, 130, 131; Cheyenne, 7, 130, Blackfeet, 130; Crow, 130, 131; Assiniboine, 130; Flathead, 130
Industrial Workers of the World, "Wobblies" (IWW), 61
Ingomar, MT, 167

Land speculators, "locators," 196
Langford, Nathaniel P., 11, 12
Last Change Gulch, 9, 10
Lavine, MT, 197
Loeber's Opera House, 167
Lumber industry, 35, 59, 60, 61, 62, 63
Lumberjacks, loggers, 59, 60, 61, 62, 63, 166

McDonald Pass, 253
Mcgill, Caroline, 166
Mad Plume, 131
Mason, Capt. R. H., 167
Miles City *Daily Star*, 255

Miles City (Milestown), MT, 2, 5, 196, 255
Miller, Fred, 2
Miller, J. K., 167
Miner's Court, 12
Minnesota, 195
Minstrel shows, 220
Missionaries, 129
Missoula, MT, 9, 61, 130, 252, 253, 245
Missouri River, 165
Model T, 252, 253
Montana Historical Society, 1
Montana Lumberman's Association, 61
Montana State University, 1
Morley, J. H., 12
Morrison, R. C., 2
Mullan Road, 11

Nevada, 9, 33
Nevada City, MT, 9
New Mexico, 94
North Dakota, 94, 195, 196
Northern Pacific Railroad, 61, 196, 197

Oklahoma, 94
"Ontario" mine, the, 34
Oregon, 9, 94
Ovando, MT, 253

Park to Park Highway, 254
Pennsylvania, 195
Philipsburg, MT, 167
Photographs; "beginnings," 5, 7; emulsions, 2, 3; glass plates, 2, 3; historical information, 1, 2, 3, 4, 5, 6, 8, 130, 220; interpretation, 6, 7; preservation, 1, 2, 3, 4, 5, 8, 129, 130, 131; roll film, 3, 6; selection, 1, 3, 7, 8
Placer mining, 10, 94
Plummer, Henry, 11
Politics as recreation, 221
Prickly Pear Creek, 10

Quartz mining, 10, 11, 62
"Railroad colonization," 196
Railroads, 11, 35, 59, 60, 62, 94, 131, 195, 196, 197, 198, 251
Ranchers, 59, 97, 197
Red Lodge, MT, 167
Reservations, 7, 130, 131
Rexford, MT, 167
Roads, 251, 252, 253, 254, 255
Rockers, 10
Rodeos, 219
Roosevelt, Theodore, 221
Russell, Charles M., 95, 219

St. Ignatius, MT, 167
Salmon Lake, MT, 253
Schools, 167
Shay locomotive, 60
Sheepmen, 93, 96, 97
Shelby, MT, 221
Sidney, MT, 131
Siedel, G. L., 255
Silver, 11, 13, 34, 35
Skalkalo, MT, 253
"Snapshot artists," 3, 5
Snow, W. M., 255
Sperry's Grade, 253
Stagecoaches, 251
Stamp mills, 10, 13
Steamboats, 11, 251
Stephensen, W. P., 255
Stevensville, MT, 62
Strikes; logging, 61, 62; mining, 61, 62
Stuart, Granville, 9
Stuart, James, 9
Sumatra, MT, 167

Taft, MT, 62
Tenis, Lloyd, 34
Texas, 94
Tourism, 253, 254
Tractors, 197
Two Dot, MT, 167

Utah Northern Railroad, 196
United States Forest Service, 63
University of Montana, 1

Vigilantes, 11, 12, 167
Virginia, 195
Virginia City, MT, 9, 167
Virginia City *Montana Post*, 167

War of the Copper Kings, 62
Washington, 9, 11
Washoe, MT, 167
Waterwagon Hill, 253
Wyoming, 94

Yeager, Red, 11
Yellowstone River, 165

Montana: Images of the Past *was composed in Paladium Roman type by B. Vader Phototypesetting of Fort Collins, Colorado and was printed on eighty pound Warren Lustro Offset Enamel Dull Cream by Pruett Press O'Hara, Inc. of Boulder, Colorado. The edition binding was furnished by Roswell Bookbinding of Phoenix, Arizona. Book design by Dianne Kedro. Dust jacket design by Jim Kifer.*